ABC's of Healthy Grieving:
Light for a Dark Journey

A Guidebook for Bereavement
From the
Department of Spiritual Wellness
Shawnee Mission Medical Center
Shawnee Mission, Kansas

Harold Ivan Smith D Min
Steven L. Jeffers, PhD

001 Shawnee Mission Medical Center Foundation

i

ISBN 1-58597-073-5

Library of Congress Control Number: 2001 130406

ABC's of Healthy Grieving:
© 2001 Shawnee Mission Medical Center Foundation
All rights reserved, including the right
to reproduce this book or portions thereof in any form.

For information contact:
Steven L. Jeffers at
Shawnee Mission Medical Center
9100 W. 74th Street
Shawnee Mission, KS 66204
(913) 676-2305

As we pass through our earthly life,

we're giving, taking, experiencing,

sharing, loving, and struggling.

We are here on a visa,

for this is not our permanent home.

Finding a quiet place

can remind us that,

after we die, we will come home

to where our passport is valid.

Malcolm Boyd, *Go Gently into That Good Night*, p. 70

Foreword

My sister, Nancy Cruzan, was involved in an automobile accident in 1983. She went without oxygen for so long that she was left in a persistent vegetative state. It took our family nearly four years to come to terms with the reality of Nan's condition, and the fact that she would never recover. Once we came to this realization, we asked ourselves what choice would Nan make about continuing a treatment, which served only to maintain her medical limbo. We all agreed Nan would choose to have the treatment stopped. We then became involved with the legal system when we asked to have the artificially supplied nutrition and hydration removed. The case went all the way to the United States Supreme Court.

On December 14, 1990, we received the court order that allowed for the removal of Nan's feeding tube. Twelve days later, on December 26, 1990, Nan peacefully passed from this life. Although we had fought for this on Nan's behalf, our family still grieved. We had tried to prepare for the loss and the grief, but I think losing someone, even when it is expected, is something you are never really prepared for.

In the years since Nan's death, my parents have also left this world behind. My dad took his own life in August 1996, and my mom succumbed to lymphoma in March 1999. With each of these losses, I have searched for guidance to help me through the grief. I have tried to find ways to adjust to the life changes brought about by the death of a loved one.

Steve Jeffers' and Harold Ivan Smith's work has brought new light to this sometimes dark and lonely journey. When I read this book, I found reinforcement for the ways in which I have been successful in dealing with my grief. I also found valuable insight for handling those areas where I have continued to struggle.

Steve understands that sitting down to read an entire book on grief can sometimes be a daunting task for those struggling through the grieving process.

His innovate solution has been to present this book so that each page begins with a particular thought in italic print, and then on the remainder of the page, he provides insightful and comforting words about that topic. This method of presentation allows the reader to approach the book in his or her own time, whether that is reading it from cover to cover or simply looking through the pages for help in a specific area.

I believe this work also provides valuable lessons to those of us who search for the right words as we attempt to offer our sympathy to someone who has experienced the loss of a loved one. After reading this book, we are left with a deeper understanding of some of the things with which a grieving person can be struggling. This insight gives us an opportunity to be more supportive to those who are grieving.

Finally, I believe giving this book as a gift to someone who has suffered the loss of a loved one would be a most appropriate way to offer support and sympathy to that grieving individual.

> Chris Cruzan White
> Cruzan Foundation
> January 2001

Editor's Preface

I would describe Harold Ivan Smith as a master "wordsmith" and storyteller who, whether speaking or writing, leads people to say: "I never quite thought of it that way before." After reading any of his books – *On Grieving the Death of a Father, A Decembered Grief: Living with Loss When Others Are Celebrating*, and others including this present work – or listening to him speak, I dare say that your assessment of him will concur with mine. However, even though it is his down-to-earth wholesomeness that endears him to many people, Harold Ivan Smith is a highly qualified, competent professional in grief work.

He is a member of the National Storytellers Network, the National Council of Hospice Professionals, Grief International, and the Association for Death Education and Counseling. Furthermore, Harold Ivan holds degrees from several colleges and universities including the Doctor of Ministry in Spiritual Formation from Asbury Theological Seminary. Moreover, he is an adjunct professor at Northern Baptist Theological seminary and has taught courses on bereavement at Nazarene Theological Seminary and Olivet Nazarene University and for the Air Force. Speaking engagements have taken him to China, Haiti, Egypt, Greece, and Israel as well as throughout the United States. His credentials are impressive to say the least.

In addition to my sincere gratitude for Harold Ivan Smith as the book's author, I am deeply appreciative of the dedication of the following individuals: Ivan Bartolome, Administrative Director of Program Development of Shawnee Mission Medical Center; Jerry Rexin, Manager of the Spiritual Wellness Department of Shawnee Mission Medical Center; Martha Rexin; Paul Ketron, Administrative Director of Facilities Management of Shawnee Mission Medical Center and Co-pastor of North Overland Park Baptist Church; and Quentin Jones, Senior Pastor of Merriam Christian Church. Each of these individuals made valuable suggestions, which were given serious consideration. Thanks to each of you for the invaluable contributions you have made to this project.

Moreover, I am grateful to Jim Boyle, Sam Turner, Robin Harrold, Sheri Hawkins, and Keith Richardson, senior administrators of Shawnee Mission Medical Center, for their valuable contributions to the success of this endeavor. Similarly, appreciation is extended to Bill Grosz and Lou Gehring, executives of Shawnee Mission Medical Center Foundation, for their unwavering confirmation of the importance of such a book. In addition, I am thankful for Bob Woolford's work of advocacy of this book's value to other hospitals throughout the United States.

Now, I want to say something about the book itself. Our intention at Shawnee Mission Medical Center in offering this book is that it would not be in textbook form (i.e., in chapter form with multiple pages per chapter). Rather, we believe that a document with short, "stand alone," single-page pearls of wisdom on the pilgrimage of grief would be more useful and helpful to grievers and those who support them. This mindset resulted in Harold Ivan Smith's ABC format. With respect to the book's organization, each page of the text begins with a letter of the alphabet (starting with the letter "A") coupled with a saying that corresponds with that letter. For example, the first page of the text proper reads like this: *A Allow for Individual Differences in Grieving Within Families.* Underneath the theme statement is at least one quote from a book, an article, or an individual, which relates to the stated theme of that page. The quote is followed by commentary, which discusses the theme. The page then concludes with an "I can" statement; the corollary to the "A" statement cited above is: *I can give each family member permission to try out grief.*

In conclusion, we at Shawnee Mission Medical Center hope that this book will be an invaluable resource for both grievers and professionals offering counsel and support to grievers. So, we encourage you to read one, two, three pages a day, reflect on them, and share them.

May your grief be healthy!

Sincerely,

Steven L. Jeffers, PhD
Community Outreach Project Coordinator
Department of Spiritual Wellness
Shawnee Mission Medical Center

I have also learned . . . through pain,

that I must be patient with myself.

Just as my body is going to need

more time to complete its healing from

the physical trauma of the accident,

so my heart, my spirit, also need time,

and I

ever impatient,

must be patient with myself.

Madeleine L. Engle, *Glimpses of Grace*, p. 210

Introduction

Death is the most permanent of facts. Death has a way of saying to even the biggest control freak, "You are *not* in control." Death whether expected or unexpected, and tragically invasive, functions like a cue ball on a rack of billiard balls: "Whack!" As the balls career wildly across the felt, the breaker scans the table and ponders, "What do we have here?"

A griever asks the same question: "What have we here?" You may have never before experienced the death of someone close. But even if you have, you have not experienced *this* death before. Even if you have expected the death after a long illness or a serious accident, grief has a way of surprising us with twists and turns, little ambushes that taunt, "Ha! You thought you were rid of me, didn't you?"

Paraphrasing a popular bumper sticker, "Grief happens." Sometimes grief just marches into our lives, taps us on the shoulder and snaps, "*You're it!*" Not unlike a tidal wave, grief spreads through family, friendships, neighborhood, and workplace relationships, touching – and sometimes wrecking – a great deal of life's shoreline. No one can change the reality of death. However, we can change the way we respond when it occurs.

Grievers must take responsibility and make decisions about whether they will go through grief or grow through the experienced loss, and either choice has long-term consequences. No few have moaned after a loved one's death, "I wish they would go ahead and bury me, too." But that is not how it works unless you make that decision. Incidentally, some individuals have died with a spouse or child's death, but the funeral was just delayed for another five or twenty-five years!

Grief is a struggle not only with the loss of a loved one but even with God or our understanding of Him. People may also struggle with family members, perhaps, or memories, influences, government bureaucracies and red tape, and more importantly, themselves.

Because of this, too many people want grief to be something that once gotten over, leaves you pretty much the same. No one who goes through grief, though, remains the same. My experience is that grievers can be wiser, more humane, more human, and more tender than before they were touched by grief. As a process within us, sometimes grief's work is very apparent; other times, it is silently conducting business.

To be sure, death has lessons to teach. I have written this book while grieving my mother's death and experiencing my first holiday season without her. I thought I knew something about grief, after all I am a professional grief educator. But I am learning that grief is a demanding tutor and, more than once, I have had my knuckles rapped and heard a stern, **"Pay attention!"**

My hope is that you will not "simply have visited" or "lightly tasted" of grief but that you will be a thorough pilgrim, not just a tourist on a tour content with seeing things from the safety of the bus. Take time to explore the side streets, the small shops, hidden gardens, and to sit and soak up the experience of some small serendipity. I am amused by those who think they have experienced Europe on one of those "seven countries in seven days" trips.

It is my earnest desire that you be blessed with the presence of those who will give you courage, for grief is an awfully big adventure for one person to manage. May there be those in your life who applaud your courage: sometimes three steps forward, sometimes two backwards. May your grief, in time, become "good grief" – however outrageous that may sound at this point on your grief path

I cannot sit with you and listen to your story, but through this book written primarily for grievers – which sooner or later will include all of us – I seek to share some of the ideas that I offer through Grief Gatherings and other workshops. *ABC's of Healthy Grieving* contains applications of ideas gained from my work with many grievers as well as insights from colleagues in the Association for Death Education and Counseling. If the grievers I have worked with could speak directly to you, they would say: "Exercise your rights; do the hard time, and grow!" My colleagues would say this, "Engage your grief!"

Admittedly, some readers will browse this book's contents seeking to gain insights into understanding the grieving behaviors of a spouse, family member, friend, neighbor, or work colleague. Others, tired of thinking, "I do not know what to do or say," will read looking for ways to support a griever. However, many will read to help themselves grieve in a healthier manner.

Finally, I hope you will dare grief, "Take your best shot." In your time of loss, give your grief its voice. Remember that your *griefprint* will be as individual as your thumbprint. Listen to your heart.

Allow grief to teach you lessons.

Harold Ivan Smith, D Min

Grief is a lot like walking along a beach
keeping one eye on the tide,
another on the sand
in order to keep our pants legs dry.
Then come the little hops we have to do, laughing,
'That one almost got me.'

Some are content to walk in the sand,
But, others take off the shoes,
roll up their pants legs, and slightly
experience the water.
Some are content to get
only their toes wet.

I do not want to be one content
with merely walking a beach or
wading in the shallow tide.

I want to be one
who experiences the water;
I want the waves to break over my head,
even if that means a mouthful of saltwater.

At last, I want to walk from the water refreshed. So
that, even after drying off and walking away,
I turn back for one last look.
I will not be content
with a lite portion of the ocean
or of grief.

Table of Contents

Foreword iv
Editor's Preface vi
Introduction ix
Grief Is a Lot Like Walking Along a Beach xii

Allow for Individual Differences in Grieving Within the Families 1
Anticipate the "Holiday Blues" 2
Ask Your Questions 3
Babystep 4
Be Sensitive to "Ex" Family Members 5
Befriend the Silence 6
Be With Your Grief 7
Breathe! 8
Create a Cherishable Memory 9
Cry 10
Decide Specific Things Friends Can Do for You 11
Discourage Hasty Decisions 12
Do the Hard Time! 13
Do the Paperwork and Ask for Help 14
Eat 15
Exercise 16
Exercise Your Rights 17
Explore New Bedtime / End-of-Day Rituals 18
Expect Some People To Be Insensitive 19
Expect Some Tough Days and Nights 20
Face Your Fears 21
Find a Safe Place To Grieve 22
Find a Skilled Counselor or Support Group 23
Finish the Unfinished Business 24
Forgive 25
Get a Massage 26
Get a Physical 27
Give Yourself Permission To Grieve 28
Go Late / Leave Early 29

"Gratitude" Your Day 30

"Help" or "Help!" Is an Important Part of a Griever's Vocabulary 31

Honor the Wishes of the Deceased if Possible 32

Include Children in the Grief 33

Innovate 34

Inventory the Promises and the Promise Makers 35

Journal Your Grief 36

Keep Pictures Out and Up 37

Know Your Limitations 38

Live Your Life Now! 39

Make Some New Traditions 40

Make Special 41

Make Your Own Funeral Wishes Known 42

Meditate 43

Name the Name 44

Never Apologize for Crying 45

Notice Your Environment 46

Observe Memorial Day 47

Overlook the Easy Answers 48

Pamper Yourself 49

Pay Attention to the Distress Signals 50

Quit Urging Yourself To "Get Over It" 51

Recognize Anniversary Grief 52

Recruit Your Support 53

Reflect on the Loss 54

Remember 55

Ritualize 56

Say It Now! 57

Sign Up for a Support Group 58

Symbolize Your Grief 59

Take Your Time 60

Tell God What Is on Your Mind 61

"Thumbs Up" Your Grief 62

Trust Your Loved One to God's Keeping 63

Update Your Estate Plan 64

Visit the Cemetery or Scattering Area 65

Write It Down 66

Write Thank-You Notes on Your Schedule 67

Xerox® Stuff 68

Yes! The Best 69

Zest Up Your Life 70

Zoom In, Zoom Out 71

Conclusion 72

When You Get Ready 73

Sources 74

Allow for Individual Differences in Grieving Within Families.

If there is one thing I have learned ... It's that we all grieve in our own ways and on our own schedule.

Candy Lightner, quoted in Shaw, *What To Do When a Loved One Dies,* p. 288

Individuals grieve at their own paces. Unfortunately, someone in the family – or outside the family – volunteers to be the "grief manager" and wants to organize, audit, and critique the grief behaviors of everyone touched by the loss: "He isn't talking," or "She hasn't cried at all since her father died."

It is essential that individuals have the freedom to "try out" their grief. Some males, for example, are influenced by the cultural notion, that they must be brave or strong. Some have been told to "Be strong . . . . for your mother, your wife . . . ." Some women feel like they have to take care of everyone and have little energy or time left to care for themselves.

Children often grieve in segments and balance being a child with it. Then some parents get uptight when children want to play with friends or by themselves. Many teens find grief an intrusion on their lives because it makes them feel different from their peers. They may retreat to their rooms and isolate themselves from other members of the family, or they may prefer to hang out with friends.

Sometimes, family members assume roles in the drama of grief, albeit some of the roles are not healthy: the strong one, the one who goes to pieces, the one who never takes anything seriously, the one who drinks to drown out his or her grief. Having said all of that though, one of the wonderful gifts of grief is the permission to confront that grief in a personal style.

I can give each family member permission to try out grief.

1

Anticipate the Holiday Blues.

No matter what your religion is, Christmas is all around you, coming at you from all directions.

Helen Fitzgerald, *The Mourning Handbook*, p. 107

"How can I possibly face this day – which is ordinary to everyone else?" Our personal calendars are dotted with special-for-us holidays that we shared with loved ones. Holidays are tough.

There are the major league holidays like Christmas, Thanksgiving, New Year's, Hanukkah, and Ramadan that have rich family significance. Valentine's Day is the romance holiday. The Fourth of July and Labor Day prompt picnics and backyard get-togethers. Memorial Day, once celebrated as Decoration Day, has become, for too many, merely the first day of summer and a time to go to the lake or the beach rather than a day to pay attention to the dead and grieving. Holidays like Mother's Day and Father's Day can be emotional nightmares for those grieving the death of a parent or those who have lost a child and no longer feel like a mom or dad. Additionally, there are those personal days like anniversaries (more than just weddings) and birthdays that are equally difficult times for grievers.

Grievers must anticipate the holiday blues. However, a holiday is an occasion to decide, "How do I want to celebrate this day **now**?" You may decide to take a sabbatical and sit it out. You may decide to do something totally different this year – something that you may never try again. In whatever way you celebrate, allow moments for grief to be front-and-center.

I can anticipate the holiday blues.

Ask Your Questions.

Questions are disturbing, especially those which may threaten our traditions, our institutions, our security. But questions never threaten the living God who is constantly calling us, and who affirms for us that love is stronger than hate, blessing stronger than cursing.

Madeleine L. Engle, *Glimpses of Grace*, p. 94

One of the ways society disenfranchises grievers is by discouraging questions. The old Southern hymn, *"We Will Understand It Better By-and-By,"* to some translates, "So don't bother to ask questions now." To others, it means, "Keep your questions to yourself, please."

But go ahead. Ask your questions. Take your best shot. Ask your tough, hard-to-phrase questions because many grievers question their way into making meaning of their losses. Questions, although not always answerable, start us down the road in the direction of answers.

Admittedly, questions that involve God -- "Why, God?!" -- make a lot of people uncomfortable, very uncomfortable. It is as natural, though, for a griever to ask that question as for a swimmer to breathe. Maybe you have seen the movie, *Steel Magnolias*, in which the mother (played by Sally Field) asks friends at the grave of her daughter, *"I want to know why?"* She concludes her outburst with, *"God, I wish I could understand."* It is not a question of asking questions, but of whom we ask, and what kind of answers we expect. In time, we **will** understand it better. For now, ask your questions and do not settle for the easy answers.

I can ask my questions.

3

 *Babystep.*

You have to crawl before you can walk. Unfortunately, we expect grievers to "get over" their grief by great leaps and bounds. We congratulate grievers, "You are handling this so well . . .," often without giving them opportunities to deny the affirmation.

Tom Hanks explains in the movie, *Sleepless in Seattle, "Well I am going to get out of bed tomorrow, and put one foot in front of the other . . ."* Amazingly, most grievers do simply put one foot in front of the other. Then at some point, they look back and realize how far they have come. Dr. Robert Schuller has rightly said, *"Inch by inch . . . . anything is a cinch."*

I can take some babysteps today.

Be Sensitive to "Ex" Family Members.

Grieving ex-spouses may feel a lack of support . . . because the deceased is no longer a family member, the ex-spouse may not be given time off from work or other special considerations, even though he or she is grieving intensely.

Alicia Skinner Cook and Kevin Ann Oltjenbruns, *Dying and Grieving*, p. 385

Divorce and death do not end relationships; they change relationships. Given the failure of one out of two marriages in this country, millions of divorced people have an ex-mate and numerous ex-in-laws. For individuals who have children from multiple marriages, all of this can create entanglements that leave Miss Manners and Ann Landers bewildered. Unfortunately, society has not worked out the details of post-divorce interaction, let alone grief, so you make it up as you go.

Sometimes, individuals may feel ambushed by grief for an ex. *"After all that went on between us, or after years have passed, how can I be grieving?"* one ex asks. It can be equally confusing if you have remarried and your spouse is wondering, *"I thought you said he was a jerk?"* Should you attend the visitation? The funeral? Send flowers? Some ex-spouses conclude, "You are damned if you go and damned if you do not go." One divorced woman explains, "I attended the funeral not as an ex-spouse, but as the mother of his children." Without question, grief can be troublesome if there are unresolved feelings or issues among individuals. However, if you attend the funeral service, remember the clergy and eulogists may focus on the present marriage and ignore your involvement in the relationship and possibly that of your children as well.

On the other hand, some people have genuine affection for ex-in-laws, particularly when she or he is a super grandparent. In cases like this, the grief is natural for wherever there is love there will be grief.

Finally, sometimes we are grieving our hopes for reconciliation. My advice is: "Listen to your heart."

I can be sensitive to "ex" family members.

Befriend the Silence.

Silence is restful: it rests the heart, the lungs, the larynx, the tongue, the lips – and the mouth.

Leo Rosen, *Treasury of Jewish Quotations*, p. 418

We're walking temples of noise . . .

Anne Lamott, *Traveling Mercies*, p. 65

Supposedly, "silence is golden." Not many grievers, though, would agree with that English proverb, for one of the most difficult tasks of many grievers is living in a silent or quiet residence. One mother, who had a long running battle with her son over the volume of music, now regrets having "stayed on him about the noise." Others confess that they miss the noises created by another person in the house: showers, toilets flushing, doors slamming, even snoring! Eating in silence can also be difficult, particularly in a nice restaurant, or watching the news without a spouse offering commentary. Additionally, habits like reading magazines or newspapers and saying, "Hey, listen to this . . ." are hard to break. Moreover, some caregivers have slept lightly for years, alert to the first sounds of distress. Now, they find it difficult to sleep in the silence. "Silent Night" is not just the name of a carol. It is a reality for many grievers.

For those reasons, it is easy to understand why grievers are tempted to drown the silence with noise. Some grievers turn on the radio or television as soon as they come home. Still others use noise to ward off hearing alarming sounds in the night. It is in the silence, though, that we hear our grief. In grief, there are things our hearts want to tell us, but they will not shout over the noise with which we fill our lives.

Befriend the silence.

I can befriend the silence.

Be With Your Grief.

*When one loses a significant other, even though there may have been
advanced warning of the death, there is always a certain sense of
unreality, a sense that it did not really happen. Therefore, the first
grief task is to come to a more complete awareness that the loss
actually has occurred, the person is dead and will not return.
Survivors must accept this reality so they can deal with the emotional
impact of the loss.*

J. William Worden, *Grief Counseling*, p. 42

One great temptation to grievers is to dodge their grief. Grieving
people find difficulty giving themselves permission to "hang out" (as
young adults say) with their grief. Grievers often hear, "Best not to
dwell on it" or "Stay busy," so they over schedule. By staying busy,
though, we miss out on the incredible wisdom grief can teach. This
wisdom can only be learned through spending time in grief's
classroom. Like news breaks on television, we need grief breaks or
time-outs.

Furthermore, some think of grief as a prison sentence to be served with
time off for good behavior. Unfortunately, those who try to avoid
doing their grief work in full will eventually face complicated grief.
For example, ignore a leak in the roof and the damage it causes may
not be immediately evident. But sooner or later, we will pay the roofer
to do repairs. Moreover, sometimes we think we are over the grief
until another death "reboots" our grief.

Finally, Susan Ford Wiltshire learned this from her brother's death:
*"When someone dies or leaves, we have to revisit in new ways the
places they inhabited in our hearts. It is not so much that we take part
of them into us, as that, in their absence, we discover or cultivate a
part of us we did not know was there. This does not compensate for
the loss. The loss is still loss, but creative healing becomes part of
their legacy to us" (Athena's Disguises, p. 134).*

Blessed are those who make space in their hearts and lives for
thorough grief.

I can "be with" my grief.

7

 *Breathe!*

Breath moves through you, in and out, twenty-two thousand times a day. Set aside some time to consciously enjoy the beauty of that flowing.

Lorin Roche, *Meditation Made Easy*, p. 182

Are you aware that grief impacts every system of the body including the respiratory system? Consequently, grievers do not always breathe well or thoroughly. Part of the reason for this has to do with improper posture: when a person slumps, the diaphragm is cut off and breathing is altered. However, when someone is depressed, as are most individuals dealing with a loss, proper posture is the last thing one would think about.

Have you ever wondered why grievers sigh? Sighing is an automatic process which says to the lungs, *"Hey, wake up in there!"* Just as we forget to eat, many of us forget to breathe. **Before you read another sentence, take a couple of deep breaths.**

Sometimes, one wise thing we can do when someone asks an offensive question or challenges our grief style is take a deep breath, a long, deep breath. Many grievers have discovered that when they breathe first, they have less for which to apologize. Furthermore, when grief settles in or "comes over me" when I feel ambushed, taking some deep breaths is a good starting point for response.

Moreover, a brisk walk and moments in fresh air will do wonders for a griever. Interestingly, that is why funeral homes once had porches or verandas.

Finally, many grievers feel that they just need some "breathing room." They may feel smothered by all the initial attention and comforting. Sometimes, the greatest gift you can give yourself … is time to breathe.

I can breathe.

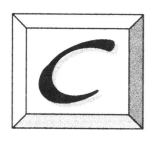

Create a Cherishable Memory.

To love and cherish, till death us do part...

Traditional wedding vows

The same promise attested in that quote might be extended after the death. One Southern gospel song is *"Precious memories . . . unseen angels."* Memories, as an inevitable result of our investment in a relationship with a person, are a friend to grievers not a menace. However, some try to keep memories at bay like a lion-tamer trying to control lions. They crack their whips and yell, "Get back!" Why is this so common? The reason is not everyone's private reality corresponds with a public perception.

On the surface, a couple appeared to have had a great relationship. Maybe at one time it was great. But by the time of the death, there had been considerable strain and repeated woundings. Furthermore, you may have been a victim of incest; your loved one may have been verbally or physically abusive when drinking; your relationship with an adult child or teen may have been strained; you may have different memories from other members of the family. But even if it was a bad relationship, there has to be something good somewhere. Relationships cannot be 100 percent bad. Sift through the relationship; identify something that was good; think about it; and then create a cherishable memory from that sliver of a memory. Wise grievers welcome memories as they would an honored guest in order to create cherishable memories. Memories happen as the following brief story indicates.

My father was a strong supporter of the Salvation Army. Even though we were poor, he passed out pennies for us to drop in the kettles during Christmas. Now, after his death, it would be easy for me to write a check to the Salvation Army and be done with it. However, I do not pass a Christmas red kettle without stopping to put something in. I find it a warm way to remember my father.

I can create a cherishable memory.

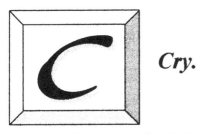

Cry.

What soap is for the body, tears are for the soul.

Leo Rosten, *Treasury of Jewish Quotations*, p. 449

I'm afraid I was pretty much of a sissy about it, cause I sat in my raft and sobbed for a while. It bothers me so very much. I did tell them, and when I bailed out I felt that they must have gone, and yet now I feel so terribly responsible for their fate, oh, so much so right now. Perhaps as the days go by it all will change and I will be able to look upon it in a different light.

George Bush, after the death of two of his crew in a plane crash in World War II, *All the Best*, p. 51

Human beings are designed to cry; crying is natural. Crying is a universal language. How many of us have said after a good cry, "I feel better now." It is one of the ways that we are "fearfully and wonderfully made." You may not hear when someone speaks, but you do "hear" a tear. Even a child will ask, "Why is she crying?"

However, many people are grief-inhibited because of admonitions from childhood: "Big boys don't cry!" or "Stop crying!" Worse than these are the lingering effects of the taunts, "Crybaby!" I would love to rewrite the old hit song, *"It's my party and I'll cry if I want to ... "* to say "It's my *grief* and I'll cry if I want to." Unfortunately, tears make many individuals uncomfortable. Act like you are going to cry and someone immediately thrusts you a tissue, which is another way of saying, "Stop crying."

Never apologize for tears. Ana Veciana-Suarez admits, *"I have designated crying areas to vent my rage and my sorrow; during my morning shower, in the car while driving alone, in the solitary confines of my home office – anywhere really where the children won't have to hear my sobs"* ("Grief Heals Slowly, But It Does Heal," p. H5). You, too, can follow Ana's example and have a designated crying area.

I can give myself permission to cry.

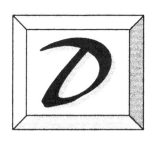 **Decide Specific Things Friends Can Do for You.**

*The Sassover Rebbe said that he learned the meaning of love from
over-hearing a conversation between two villagers.
One asked the other, 'Do you love me?'
The second replied, 'I love you deeply.'
The first asked, 'Do you know, my friend, what gives me pain?'
The second protested that he could not possibly know.
'If you do not know what gives me pain,' lamented the first,
'how can you say you love me?'*

David Wolpe, *Making Loss Matter*, pp.148-149

Can you receive? Can you take someone up on an offer, or repeated offers, to help? Sit down and make a list of things that need to be done. Now ask yourself this: "Who can best do this or fulfill this need? Who can best help me?" Then ask that person for help.

I find that a shared task promotes conversations, during or afterwards. Both the requester and the helper are enriched by the experience. So, let people in on your grief.

Decide something specific people can do for you.

*I can decide specific things that friends
can do for me.*

11

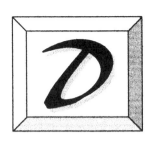

Discourage Hasty Decisions.

Haste makes Waste.

Anonymous

Listen carefully when someone is trying to talk you into doing something. Ask, "Is this decision something family members or I could long regret?" Consider one father's haste. He boxed up the good china and crystal and gave it to the Salvation Army. Days later in a phone conversation when a daughter asked, "What have you been up to? he answered, "Oh, just getting rid of some of your mother's things." "Such as?" the daughter asked. When he answered, she gasped, "Dad, that was not just mother's -- That was ours! She would have wanted us (the daughters) to have had it." The daughter raced to the Salvation Army, found the china, and purchased it.

Few of us make good decisions under pressure – how much more so in a time of grief, particularly after an unanticipated death. The reasons for hasty decisions in grief situations are many and varied. Some individuals function from a "take charge" frame of mind. "Just do it." "Get over it." On the other hand, someone may be pressuring: "You need to do this, this and this. . . now!" Others launch into giving away items or boxing up the possessions of the loved one, motivated by the mind set, "Out of sight, out of mind." Still others can be very pragmatic: "Got to do it sometime, might as well be now."

Grief counselors advise widows and widowers, "Make no major decisions for the first year. Focus on your grief work." This is wise advice for **all** grievers. Sometimes haste cannot so easily be redeemed. If in doubt about a decision, **wait**. Sometimes, five minutes is enough to make an appropriate decision, sometimes, it takes much longer. **Do not be in a hurry.**

I can give myself time and space to make good decisions.

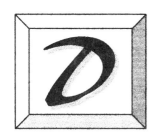

Do the Hard Time!

Here's what I've learned about grief: It's not linear, it's not predictable. It's anything but smooth and self-contained. Someone did us all a grave injustice by implying that mourning has a distinct beginning, middle and end.

Hope Edelman, *"Grief Has No Beginning,"* p. 723

Some grievers do not want grief to be demanding, inconvenient, or to mess up their priorities. Many want a parole or early release. Business people may think of it as a "buy out." We live in a culture that prefers lite beer, lite cheesecake, and lite grief. Although television, other forms of media, and increasingly, real life are saturated with death and dying, we resist talking about it. One university dean says that death is the only taboo topic at faculty gatherings on his campus.

One thing I find interesting is that Mitch Albom's *Tuesdays with Morrie* has been on *The Publishers Weekly* bestseller list for over two years and became a made-for-television movie. Maybe we really *do* want someone to talk to us about death without all the syrupy sentimentality. Maybe we want someone to tell us that dying is hard work and that grieving can even be harder work.

Because grief is hard work, we need companions for the pilgrimage through grief. The Spanish call those who accompany grievers *acompanero* or *acompana*. **A companion listens all the way to the end of our silences as well as to the end of our sentences**. Sometimes, when people tell me they are already over their grief, I want to ask, "Did you ever begin?" In math, the shortest distance between two points is a straight line. But in grief, the best route may be circuitous, at times baffling, and most certainly hard.

I can do hard time.

Do the Paperwork and Ask for Help.

Now, in addition to all the coaching he does as defensive coordinator at Kansas State, he (Phil Bennett) finds himself . . . every morning, sitting under the dining room chandelier, deciphering fine print, signing documents, making calculations, cutting fat, balancing numbers. There are so many forms, a bottomless pile, each as mysterious and elusive as a Greek poem. Three months have passed . . . .

Joe Posnanski, "Coping and Coaching," pp. C_1, C_{10}

In listening to the stories of participants in the Grief Gatherings, I have come to learn that one way our culture distances itself from death is through the layers of bureaucracy and paperwork. It is not simply that your loved one died. That death has to be officialized and notarized. Many a griever has served as executor of the estate of a loved one. That can become a nightmare if the loved one died without a will, had an invalid will, or a will that does not account for present circumstances and realities such as a recent marriage.

Now at a person's death, the paperwork starts with the obituary. Sometimes little factual errors in this small newspaper article can annoy or anger people. For example, someone may be left out or someone in the family may want certain things, such as the cause of death, unmentioned. Then, there are some people who reroute their anger toward the person who "messed up" the obituary.

It is in the more complicated paperwork, though, that the stress is greater. However, there is no need for you to fear. Those who have been down the path are available to offer counsel through the legal, financial, and emotional maze. When you run up against something in the paperwork that doesn't seem logical, ask for help.

I can do the paperwork and ask for help.

Eat.

*You need to eat as well as you can. Meals that you used to
look forward to may now lack appeal. Cooking, perhaps
something you used to enjoy, may have turned into drudgery
. . . If you find you can't eat three regular meals each day,
try five small ones. But avoid nibbling on junk food such as
potato chips, candy, or cookies, as these could lead to excess
weight, which will only complicate your situation.*

Helen Fitzgerald, *The Mourning Handbook*, p. 76

"I am not hungry!" are common words of grievers, even though there
may be a kitchen full of food lovingly prepared by friends and family.
Despite the admonition, "You've got to keep up your strength," many
grievers simply "forget" to eat. That is one reason that weight loss –
even malnutrition – is common among the grieving. There are other
reasons grievers do not eat. Some hate eating alone at home. Others
hate eating alone in restaurants.

One thing you will have to do, though, is master the art of eating alone.
You will also have to decide what to do about favorite restaurants. For
instance, you may not be up to going there for a while; you may decide
to go for only a salad and coffee, rather than a full meal. On the other
hand, others find a favorite restaurant to be a place where they can
remember. To declare, though, "I will never eat there again" will only
compound your grief.

Finally, concerning what and how you eat, you may wisely limit your
intake of foods containing caffeine, which interferes with sleep. Eat
more fresh fruits, which are easier for a grieving body to digest. Also,
carefully monitor your intake of snack foods. It is very tempting to
snack and nibble rather than to prepare a full meal. It is equally
important to monitor the eating habits of other family members
because it is possible to go in the opposite direction and use food as a
numb-er to avoid feelings.

Even in grief, I can eat healthily.

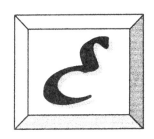

Exercise.

Exercise, always important to good health, is even more important now . . . regular exercise can help reduce that stress, discharging anger or frustration.

Helen Fitzgerald, *The Mourning Handbook*, p. 244

Deep within our brains are barracks filled with wonderful substances called endorphins. (Think of Richard Simmons, and you are halfway to understanding their function.) When we exercise, endorphins are released into the bloodstream, and they dash up and down the corridors of our bodies screaming, "Party Time!!!" This is why we feel so much better after a walk or a work-out. So, even if you do not feel strong, find some form of exercise. Helen Fitzgerald suggests, *"Find an exercise you enjoy doing and work it into your schedule"* (p. 244). Even if it is a spirited walk through a mall (unless you stop at Mrs. Fields for more than one cookie) or a brisk walk through the neighborhood, exercising is a way of honoring your grief.

I can find a form of exercise.

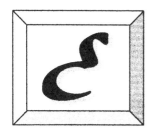

Exercise Your Rights.

If life experiences are not used – they are wasted.

Charlotte Hullinger, quoted in Schlosser, "A Grief Like No Other," p. 50

My colleague, Dr. Alan Wolfelt suggests that grievers have "rights," which, if exercised responsibly, lead to reconciliation with the death(s) (*The Journey Through Grief,* pp. 141-142).

As a Griever I have the right to

❖ Experience my own unique grief

❖ Talk about my grief

❖ Feel a multitude of emotions

❖ Be tolerant of my physical, emotional, and financial limits

❖ Experience "grief bursts" of pain and anxiety

❖ Make use of additional ritual

❖ Embrace my spirituality

❖ Search for meaning

❖ Honor my memories

❖ Move toward my grief and to heal

I can exercise my rights.

Explore New Bedtime / End-of-Day Rituals.

We are all creatures of our end-of-day routines. For some busy people, that is when they have time for themselves or time for a spouse. It may also mean a quality, special time with a child – hearing about the day, telling a favorite story, or listening to prayers. Furthermore, for many adults, bedtime is associated with sexual intimacy, whether intercourse or cuddling and talking. Now, a half-empty bed can be an incredible reminder of loss. In fact, the loss of a sleeping companion or sexual partner and a good night's sleep, for many, is a secondary loss. (The primary loss is the death of the spouse.) "I wake up exhausted."

Because of this, some find the end of the day to be the most difficult time to deal with grief. Therefore, many people simply try to stay so busy throughout the day that they will be exhausted and drop into bed and, they hope, fall asleep.

Many others delay going to bed. Some fall asleep in a favorite chair watching television or reading. But a chair is not the most comfortable sleeping environment. Therefore, many grievers end up sleep deprived, which interferes with rest, and the lack of rest interferes with grief work. This fatigue also carries over into the workplace or school.

What can you do? Sleep in a guest room or change rooms with another family member. Eliminate listening to the late news. Try a long soak or a glass of warm milk. Ask God to give you sleep. Try repeating the child's prayer, "Now I lay me down to sleep . . ."

I can explore some new bedtime / end-of-day rituals.

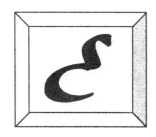

Expect Some People To Be Insensitive.

'Sticks and stones may break my bones, but words . . .'
may get stuck in the corridors of my memory.

Harold Ivan Smith

At the first meeting of Grief Gatherings, I ask, "What is the stupidest or most insensitive thing anyone has said to you?" After some people have responded, the participants moan, groan, laugh, roll their eyes, and smack their foreheads in disgust: "I cannot believe anyone actually said that to you!"

Unfortunately, many individuals do not know what to say to grievers because they have not been personally exposed to grief. Therefore, they will not have had an apprenticeship in which to learn sensitivity. So, they may ask you outrageous questions. Still, what they say or ask may ricochet through your mind and heart long afterwards like time-released medicine. One widow, only hours after her husband had died, was asked, "Well, do you think you will get married again?" And the questioner stood waiting for a response. A couple, having lost their first baby, was told, "Oh you're young. You'll have another baby ..."

Many times, however, the question, comment, or observation did not come out the way it was intended. Wise grievers advise, "Forgive them." One mother remarks, "At least they are saying something even if it is bizarre. The silence hurts me." On the other hand, a griever always has an option of being gracious and ignoring the comments. But the griever also has an option of seizing the *faux pas* as a teaching moment. By honestly describing how you feel at that moment, you may acquaint the speaker with a level of understanding that will prevent a reoccurrence with another griever. You may be doing him a favor by simply saying, "Let me tell you how that sounds to me." Moreover, there is the incredible belief that someone ought to say "something" more than "I am sorry." Furthermore, it is really difficult to hear, "Oh, I know what you are going through" because even if the individual has lost someone, she has not lost **this** someone.

I can expect some people to be insensitive.

19

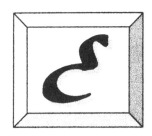

Expect Some Tough Days and Nights.

I wish someone could reassure me that it is not outrageously illogical to believe the sun will rise again, and that someday I will, after too many tough days and nights, laugh again.

Pat, participant in a Grief Gathering

In some cases, the death of a loved one is a welcome relief. "She has suffered so much physically, and the family emotionally." Perhaps some of the family has traveled both during the illness and for the funeral. Friends have dropped in constantly. Eventually, though, family members have to return to jobs, and friends return to their normal routines. However, grief goes on for the primary griever who must now become comfortable with the absence of a loved one and with reduced support.

Maybe you have had the experience of falling asleep on a couch, then waking up and saying, "Oh, it's late. I've got to go to bed." But once in bed, suddenly you were wide awake. Grief seems more intrusive at night. After my father died, my mother repeatedly told me. "The nights are the worst." That can be especially true during winter months when it gets dark earlier. Some days seemingly have more than twenty-four hours, and some hours surely have more than sixty minutes.

Grief has a way of interrupting or ambushing even the best day. Everything was going well, then suddenly out of nowhere, grief sabotaged the day. Couples looking forward to a first baby now walk by a closed door of what was to have been the nursery. What was to be turns into sleepless nights and more questions. Expect some tough days. Expect some rough nights. Sometimes there is no rhyme or reason why. It just is. The punch line for *Candid Camera* had it about right: "Sometime, when you least expect it..."

I can expect some tough days and nights.

20

Face Your Fears.

*You gain strength, courage and confidence by every
experience in which you really stop to look fear in the face.
You are able to say to yourself, 'I lived through this horror.
I can take the next thing that comes along. . .'
You must do the thing you think you cannot do.*

Eleanor Roosevelt, quoted in Bartlett, p. 876

Structurally, fears are like icebergs: about ten percent above the water line, which can be seen, with the lethal ninety percent lurking below. Fears are a major element in grief. The question, "How will I ever survive without . . .?" ricochets continuously down the canyons of the heart, especially for those who have lost a loved one through murder, suicide, gang violence, or in an automobile accident in which there was no warning of approaching death. If a loved one was killed in a traffic accident, just riding in a car may provoke fears and heighten anxiety.

For many grievers, the menacing fear is an ill-stated but well-known, "I will never be happy again" or "my life is over." Some fear being alone for the rest of their lives, while others fear the death of another loved one. Fear often launches the "poor me" symphony.

A griever's fears often have consequences for other family members. Mamie Eisenhower, whose son Ikky died in 1921 of scarlet fever, was so afraid that her son John would die that she hovered over him. This made for a tough childhood.

Nothing is wrong with having fears – it is what you do with those fears that counts. I like the slogan on a tee-shirt: **"Feel the fear and do it anyway!"**

I can face my fears.

Find a Safe Place To Grieve.

For me, the safe place is the cemetery.
For me, it's my bedroom. I put one of those motel
'Do not disturb' signs on the door and everyone
knows to leave me alone.
My deck, I just sit by the hour and watch the
flowers and the squirrels.

Participants in Grief Gatherings

Grievers quickly discover that there are safe spaces and there are unsafe places to grieve. Some places one would expect to offer safety are, in fact, unsafe. One young woman, whose child had died, had to act in her home as if everything was upbeat. On the year anniversary of the child's death, her husband said, "I don't ever want to hear his name again!"

Similarly, most people find that they cannot safely grieve in their workplaces. The colleagues who sent the flowers and signed the beautiful card may be "unavailable" to listen to the griever who is having a difficult day six months after the death. Also, some find their faith communities to be unsafe after the initial period of grief. "You should be over it by now," a parishioner suggests, which unfortunately sounds like scolding.

Alternatively, you may find a support group to be that safe place. You may find telephone hot lines a safe place to give grief a voice. A kitchen table in a friend's home may become a safe place. Others go to a shared space – a place the deceased fondly enjoyed.

Grievers might create those safe spaces in their homes. One family identified a particular chair as a "designated grief zone." When feeling grief keenly, family members could sit in that chair and have their grief "timeout" honored. Photo albums were on a table next to the chair as well as a candle and matches. Look for or create your safe place.

I can find or make a safe place to grieve.

Find a Skilled Counselor or Support Group.

A support group is a healthy, safe place for you who are grieving to bring yourselves, your stories, your anger, and your bewilderment, and to know that it's just likely that others will have been there and will recognize in your story parts of their story. And it is possible that something in your story will encourage another griever in the group.

Harold Ivan Smith, *Death and Grief*, p.4

Because individualism is highly prized in American society, some grievers and some clinicians see grief as evidence of weakness. That is why individuals commonly parrot, "Be strong." However, few grievers are strong enough to do grief well without support, either from individuals, from professional helpers, or from support groups.

Admittedly, not every counselor or psychologist is skilled in the areas of grief, which result from trauma, disaster, or violence. Some counselors may even make grievers feel uncomfortable. Then, some counselors have not had first-hand experiences with loss. Others, still uphold the notions of the "stages" of grief and insist on one goal for therapy: you getting over the grief.

Ask counselors what kinds of personal losses they have experienced. Also, ask what kind of experiences they have had working with grieving people.

Most professional counselors, though, are competent and offer safety and confidentiality. Never feel bad about enlisting the support of a professional or by participating in a support group. Because clinicians have companioned others walking the path of grief, they may be particularly equipped to help you.

I can and will look for a skilled counselor or support group.

Finish the Unfinished Business.

I cannot imagine living with this load of unfinished business.
But with all that's gone on, I don't know where to begin.

Ann, participant in a Grief Gathering

Death may bring the unfinished business in our lives to a boil. Death has a way of reigniting family feuds. In fact, death makes shambles of our plans, priorities, and calendars. Many grievers have been devastated by the timing of a loved one's death, especially if it follows an argument, a long series of arguments, estrangement, or when death occurs after a relationship has improved or a relational hurdle has been eliminated. "We went through so much . . . then this. **Why now?**" The reality is that even in the best relationships, unfinished work may remain.

You may have unfinished business with a person who has died. If so, it is beneficial to honestly acknowledge the reality of that relationship and to talk candidly about it. You might need the aid of professionals who offer perspective, particularly when there are aspects of a relationship or incidents that you do not want others to know about or even that you have denied. Some find that writing about the unfinished business is a helpful starting point. No few have written letters and then read them aloud at the cemetery, the mausoleum, or a scattering area. It may not do the deceased any good, but it does the griever a great deal of good.

Unfortunately, some things are unchangeable. However, focus on the things you can change. Morrie Schwartz, whose experience of dying was captured in the bestseller, *Tuesdays with Morrie*, insisted, *"Make peace. You need to make peace. You need to make peace with yourself and everyone around you"* (p. 167).

I can finish the unfinished business in my life.

 *Forgive.*

All that I ought to have thought and have not thought,
All that I ought to have said and have not said,
All that I ought to have done and have not done,
All that I ought not to have thought and yet have thought,
All that I ought not to have spoken and yet have spoken,
All that I ought not to have done and yet have done,
For thoughts, words, and works, I pray for forgiveness
and repent with penance.

Wayne Lee Jones, *Weave Garments of Brightness*, p. 29

Some people find it is easier to deal with a death if there is someone to blame, even if that someone is yourself. Little wonder that grievers voice the lament, "How can I forgive _____ for _____?" Forgiveness is important work for a griever. Forgiveness and grief go together like sweet and sour or salt and pepper.

Sometimes, forgiveness has to be granted to a doctor who failed to diagnose correctly. Sometimes, forgiveness has to be extended to a person who is thought responsible: a murderer (known or unknown), the driver of the other automobile (particularly if that driver was drunk, speeding, or ran a red light).

Some have to forgive the deceased not just for dying but for invoking the grief season on a family. Some have to forgive the deceased for not making a will, for not taking care of themselves, or for ignoring doctor's restrictions. Some have to forgive the friends who encouraged the drugs, drinking, or risk taking.

We must forgive those who failed to visit during a long illness. Sometimes, we must forgive family members who distanced themselves or did not meet our expectations for support. Forgiving is a decision we keep making. Forgiving is "for giving." It releases us from the exhausting work of lugging around a grudge like homeless people carrying their belongings.

With God's help, I can forgive.

Get a Massage.

*Human touch from a qualified therapist can nourish the
soul like nothing else in this world.
We touch children when they are hurt, we give them hugs
and kiss them when they cry, but we don't do it for adults.*

Mitch Finley, *101 Ways to Nourish Your Soul*, p.125

A massage is not a luxury but a basic necessity for the grieving. According to Carolyn Kresse Murray in "Getting in Touch," (p. 32h), a massage:

- ❖ Increases circulation of the blood
- ❖ Removes toxins by increasing the action of the lymphatic systems
- ❖ Increases the absorption of carbohydrates in the intestines
- ❖ Brings more blood and more oxygen to the joints and takes away carbon dioxide
- ❖ Removes metabolic waste
- ❖ Removes uric acid in joints and mucous in the lungs
- ❖ Aids in elimination

In giving loving care to your loved one during the long illness, you may have lifted, tugged, and pulled. During such times, many caregivers overlooked their own health and discounted their own need for recreation and relaxation. Now, though, is the time to make room for loving, healthy self-care. The power of a trained healthy touch can go a long way in healing your body from the prolonged psychological stress of watching a loved one die, or of going through grief. We all store our grief somewhere in our bodies: the neck, the shoulders, or the lower back. A massage is a way to address that reality.

Remember, a massage is not a luxury but an investment in your health.

I can see a massage as an investment.

Get a Physical.

*Go ahead and insult your body. It will seek and find its
ultimate revenge.
Don't expect your doctor to be a mind reader.
Tell him you are grieving.*

Attributed to Fritz Perls

Do not skip this page. "When is the last time you had a physical?"
Answer the question, please. Caregiving is an incredible stressor as is
grief. Every emotion we have translates into some type of biochemical
reaction in our bodies. Nurses are not surprised when some caregivers,
following repeated hospitalizations of loved ones, become patients
after their deaths. Sometimes, in fatigue and in grief, we ignore the
body until it dramatically gets our attention. Although you may
paraphrase Helen Reddy, "I am caregiver . . . hear me roar!" your body
deserves attention now.

Your family has already had one loss. Do not give them another. Pay
attention to your body. Take care of it through this long season called
grief.

*I can take care of my body.
I will schedule a physical.*

Give Yourself Permission to Grieve.

The problem will also be that you may not give yourself time to recover. You may be the greatest source of pressure. It may be you who feels your faith is not strong if you are not well in a period of weeks. It may be you who tries to take your grief away.

Doug Manning, *Don't Take My Grief Away*, p. 66

Some of us grew up in families that didn't handle grief well. "In this family we do not express our emotions – let alone grief!" We were trained well to respond with the stiff upper lip (even if it occasionally quivered).

Some grievers are so busy responding to the grief of others, or managing the grief of others, that they do not take time or give themselves permission to grieve. Ever said: "I have got to be strong for . . .?" I worry about the grief manager – the take-charge person. Remember Sally Field in *Steel Magnolias* standing in solitude at the casket of her daughter, then talking with her friends. Suddenly, she announces, *"I have to get back . . .I have things to do."* Society places great responsibility on women to be caregivers to the dying and the living and, in essence, to function as grief managers to the grieving. Ask a griever how she is doing and she may answer, "I am managing."

Some grievers are managing but exhausted and will soon find themselves in bed or ill. **Without ignoring the needs of others, particularly children, give yourself permission to do thorough, unapologetic grief and to receive care.** You are the only "you" you have, and you are the only "you" your children have.

Remember this: When you give yourself permission to grieve, you are modeling good grief to others who, sooner or later, will face this experience.

I can give myself permission to grieve.

Go Late, Leave Early.

Movement can only happen when you begin to assume responsibility for yourself and say, 'I won't' instead of 'I can't.' You may say 'I won't' because of some very good reasons, but to say, 'I can't' is to play the role of victim.

Doug Manning, *Don't Take My Grief Away*, p. 114

I want, at least, to be in places where joy is happening. Then, if there are any extras, I can take a 'doggy bag' full of joy home with me for tomorrow.

Bill, grieving his wife and two children killed in an automobile accident

Life goes on while we are in grief. Parties, showers, receptions, retirement celebrations, and open houses are still on. Inevitably, particularly in the business and professional world, invitations come for events in which participation may be expected, if not required. Moreover, someone may be prodding, "You've got to get out. It will do you good to be with people."

What should we do with the invitation, particularly an invitation from individuals who have been good to us since our loved one's death? Joan Rivers, from her experience as a widow, advises grievers, *"go late and leave early." "Besides,"* she adds, *"unless you are the paid entertainment, no one expects you to be the life of the party"* (Lecture, 1996, 15 May).

I can always go late and leave early.

"Gratitude" Your Day.

*No matter how trapped in the Krazy Glue of life you may
be feeling, you can get unstuck.
My favorite way is to make a list of all that I have to be
thankful for.*

Joan Rivers, *Bouncing Back*, p. 66

Irving Berlin offers therapeutic advice to grievers in the lyrics of his classic, *"And I fall asleep counting my blessings . . ."* Gratitude is an attitude, a choice. The more we practice gratitude the more it becomes part of our lives and part of our grief.

You may react, "What have I got to be grateful for? My ___ (son/wife/daughter/husband/nephew/grandchild) is dead, and you are suggesting that I ought to be grateful?" Yes, you can be grateful not for the death, but for the relationship that you had with that person, grateful that such love could exist between two human beings.

You can be grateful

❖ For the care of nurses, physicians, orderlies, and aides

❖ If you had a chance to finish unfinished business

❖ If you had a chance to say good-bye

❖ If your loved one died a peaceful death

❖ For a last kiss or smile or hug

❖ For the support of family, friends, of colleagues, or even…

❖ Of strangers you have encountered

Every day, find something for which to be grateful.

Today I can be grateful for _____.

"Help" or "Help!" Is an Important Part of a Griever's Vocabulary.

You can't stay in your corner of the forest waiting for others to come to you.
You have to go to them sometimes.

Pooh, *Pooh's Little Instruction Book*, p. 51

"My, you are handling this so well" is a compliment that many grievers like to hear. In an age that so prizes self-sufficiency, to admit needing help makes one feel vulnerable. Admittedly, many people offered help at the visitation, funeral, or even in the first days afterward, but for some it was a cliché. They never expect the coupon to be redeemed.

The angriest participant in my grief group demanded, "I just want to know one thing. Where are all the people who made all the promises at the casket?" There were quick "seconds" from other participants. "Yeah, I'd like to know that, too." One woman quickly responded, "Have you asked for help? Perhaps you've given off signals that you are handling it all by yourself." A spirited discussion then followed.

People are incredibly busy with their own priorities and schedules. Sometimes, we routinely preface requests with, "I hate to bother you," but expect, "Oh, it's no bother." By asking, though, you are doing individuals a favor by giving them a practical, tangible way to reach out to you. By lowering the drawbridge to let helpers into your grief, you may be offering the equivalent of an apprenticeship for their inevitable season of grief. So get used to the word "Help." Sometimes, it is best punctuated with exclamation marks. "Help!!!"

I can say "Help" or "Help!"

Honor the Wishes of the Deceased if Possible.

I promise I will remember what you requested.

Mary Pipher, *Another Country*, p. 204

Some families can take comfort in knowing "we tried everything there was to do" or in making funeral plans "we did the best we could . . . at the time." Missy Bernall knew that her daughter would not want a pink casket or any pink roses. Yet, when she went for the viewing, she discovered the lining of the casket was pink! *We debated having it replaced with a different color, but then, since we were going to close the casket anyway, we decided to leave it as it was. At times like that you don't know whether to laugh or cry. I managed to laugh. But I also promised her, as she lay there, that I had done my best. I tried. (She said "Yes," p. 34).*

Honoring the wishes of a deceased loved one can be a tough decision. You may have had to make a decision on "heroic measures" that you now are second guessing. "Did I do the right thing?" Other family members may have disagreed with the decision, but you acted as you did out of respect for your loved one's wishes. Sadly, many adults have never told their loved ones their wishes for end-of-life measures or rituals.

However, it is best, if possible, to follow the wishes of the deceased, with one exception. If the loved one requested "No services," that should be considered. Funerals and memorial services benefit the living and aid closure. Admittedly, some have never experienced a "good" funeral or memorial service and that most likely motivated the request, "No services." Whatever the situation, you will need to create some type of good-bye ritual, while at the same time giving consideration to the loved one's wishes.

I can honor the wishes of the deceased whenever possible.

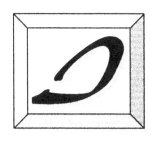

Include Children
in the Grief.

Children's questions should be answered in a straightforward direct fashion, and in terms of the family's shared beliefs regarding family roles, separation, death or the afterlife. If children are old enough to formulate questions about these losses, they are old enough to deserve appropriate answers.

Robert Neimeyer, *Living with Loss*, p. 42

Rightly or wrongly, we did not tell six-year old Georgie (George W. Bush) that his sister was dying. We hated that, but we felt it would have been too big a burden for such a little fellow.

Barbara Bush, *Barbara Bush: A Memoir*, p. 44

One of the most destructive trends in this country over the last several decades has been the exclusion of children from dying and from the rituraling. "Oh, it would only upset them." This trend is not new as evidenced in the example of the Bushes not telling their son his sister was dying. When excluded, children create explanations, some of which will be more destructive than the truth could ever be.

How old should a child be to be included? "Old enough to love, old enough to grieve." Remember, though, that a child grieves as a child and not as a miniature adult. Thus, they may be grieving one moment and running off to play the next. **Give children permission to do their grief without too many boundaries.**

Furthermore, it is helpful to explain what the child will see or experience at the funeral home or at a memorial service. Some parents take a child for part of the visitation or part of the funeral. A child may not be able to comprehend the finality of death, but a child will know that his environment has changed – perhaps radically: "My mommy cries a lot . . my daddy is sad all the time and doesn't want to play with me." You can give children permission to grieve by listening and honestly answering their questions.

I can include children in grief.

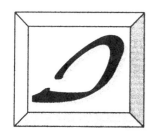

Innovate.

Sometimes, through tears, the grieving must say as sad a good-bye to traditions as they have to the people with whom they have shared those traditions.

Harold Ivan Smith, *The Gifts of Christmas*, pp. 56-57

Ask people about why they do something or observe a tradition, and they may answer, "Oh, we've just always done it this way." We can become prisoners to traditions that long ago lost their lives and vitality. Grievers are "creatures of habit." Some believe their loved one would not approve of any change of tradition.

One father decided to "make it up to the boys for all they had been through" by preparing the traditional Thanksgiving feast. Unfortunately, he had never baked a turkey before and had no idea what he was in for (neither did his sons). He peeled off the wrapper and stuck the bird in the oven and waited and waited while his sons munched on peanut butter sandwiches and popcorn. By his own admission, that first Thanksgiving was a disaster. Wisely, the next year his sons convened a family council and vetoed the idea of a repeat performance. They agreed the one item their dad could cook was chili. So, they innovated with a chili dinner at high noon on Thanksgiving.

Maybe you or your late spouse had different ideas about holidays and spending and decorating. Now, you have a free hand to do it "your" way. Jettison the guilt, and innovate. It may well end up as not only "This works for me," but as a meaningful new tradition.

I can innovate.

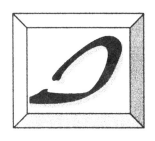

Inventory the Promises and the Promise Makers.

Hold no man responsible for what he says in his grief.

Leo Rosten, *Treasury of Jewish Quotations*, p. 384

What we have here is a failure to communicate.

Donn Pearce, *Cool Hand Luke*, quoted in Bartlett, p. 908

Art Linkletter thought kids say the darnedest things, but if he had spent much time in funeral homes, he would have expanded his horizons. Caskets cause people to say and to promise the darnedest things: "You just call me if there is anything I can do," and some add "**Anything at all**." Some repeat the promise. Some even punctuate the promise with a smile, a hug, or a squeeze.

Realistically, promises have a short shelf life. Promise makers forget. Some promise makers never expect you to "cash in" the promise.

But some promise makers can help you. How do you figure out who they are?

❖ Take a moment to think about what you need.
❖ Take a moment to think about when you need it done.
❖ Take a moment to think about whom can best fulfill that need.
❖ Take a moment to "boot-up" courage.

Now, call that individual. Admittedly, it may be necessary to remind them, "Remember, when you said at the funeral home that if there was anything I needed I could call? Well, I thought of something." Like tennis, the ball is now in his court.

I can ask individuals to help me in specific ways.

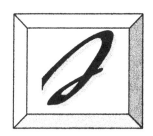

"Journal" Your Grief.

A journal is not only a record of events that touch and transform us; it is a private space in which we can meet ourselves in relationship to others and to God.

Susan A. Muto, *Pathways of Spiritual Living*, pp. 94-95

Journal writing is for me a form of prayer . . . Talking to paper was the only way I knew to talk to God, and it proved to be an ideal form of prayer because it gave me a way to see what was going on in my heart.

Renita J. Weems, *Listening for God*, p. 54

Journaling can be summed up like this: "Write it down" or "write it out." You may think, "Oh, I will never forget . . .," but you will. There are so many competing thoughts, responses, and coincidences that only by taking time to "be with" and write down your thoughts can you process them.

Admittedly, some of our thoughts are menacing, even accusatory, but by writing them down on paper in black and white, we can encounter them and, with God's help, diffuse them. In a journal, you can respond in a way that you could never respond verbally. Journals are a venue for the brutal honesty that is a part of good grief work. Renita Weems insists that journals give grievers *"some place to tell the truth"* (p. 56). What we first explore on a journal page, we may, in time, be able to disclose to another family member, friend, minister, or clinician.

Initially, you may be at a loss for words. Try one of these jump-starters.

Grief came knocking at my door one day. . .
I keep thinking that one of these days. . .
I have been surprised by the intensity of my feelings about. . .

I can "journal."

Keep Pictures Out and Up.

Last year I looked at the photos on the piano and realized that it was turning into the memorial Steinway: Edgar, my mother, my father . . . Although I got rid of none of those bittersweet photos, I did add many new ones to remind me that life goes on . . . Now instead of depressing me, that piano is a tableau of my life, good times and bad.

Joan Rivers, *Bouncing Back,* p.154

"I can't look at the pictures . . . too many memories" is a common quotation heard in Grief Gatherings. Some take an "out of sight, out of mind" approach. Thus, one of the first items of the agenda is to put away the pictures. Unfortunately, this action tends to be counterproductive because the mind remembers where pictures used to be. In an attempt to reverse that mind set, at the last session of every Grief Gathering group, I request that participants bring photos of their respective loved ones for other members of the group to see. My intent in so doing is to encourage people to "keep these pictures out and up."

After my father's death, my mother told me that she often talked to his picture when she was distressed. No doubt, she even kissed those pictures from time to time. The pictures offered her a link.

Her experience was radically different from that of Theodore Roosevelt who destroyed every picture of his first wife, Alice, after her death on Valentine's Day, 1884. Little wonder he exclaimed, *"The light has gone out in my life"* (Morris, *The Rise of Theodore Roosevelt,* p. 241).

Pictures can be a bittersweet experience, but most people find them a necessary resource for doing grief work thoroughly.

I can keep the pictures out and up.

Know Your Limitations.

"I don't think I am up to it, but it's good of you to ask . . .maybe next time." Those are frequent words of the grieving. In a culture that expects life to go on, you will be asked to social events, to take part in celebrations as if nothing has happened. Once, widows declined social invitations for a year and then returned to social life.

Doug Manning in his wonderful book, *Don't Take My Grief Away*, urges grievers to acknowledge their limitations. *"If you had a broken leg, no one would criticize you for using crutches until it was healed. If you had major surgery, no one would pressure you to run in a marathon next week. You must have the time and the crutches until you heal"* (p. 65). Grief, like any major wound, does not heal overnight. Unfortunately, we do not enfranchise grievers to recognize and defend their limitations.

Someone offered this advice: "Do what you can -- not what you cannot." You must listen to your heart. Practice your "I don't think so" or "Let me think about it."

I can recognize and honor my limitations.

Live Your Life Now!

Devote yourself to loving others, devote yourself to your community around you, and devote yourself to creating something that gives you meaning and purpose.

Morrie Schwartz, quoted in Albom, *Tuesdays with Morrie*, p. 127

"What am I supposed to do now?" "How am I supposed to live without her . . .without him?" or in multiple losses, "without them?" I commonly hear such questions from grievers. Furthermore, it should come as no surprise that our culture has just the right response for such moments, "Life must go on." Perhaps you remember the scene in the movie *Shadowlands* when C. S. Lewis attends the first faculty gathering after the death of his wife. He is immediately confronted by an academician offering this advice, *"Life must go on, Jack."* Lewis responds dryly, *"I don't know if it must but it certainly does."*

Moreover, often grievers give veto power to a deceased mate. "He wouldn't want me to..." Then, some, who have been in unhealthy marriages, come to life after a spouse's death and yet experience regret about the new opportunities life offers. For example, one widow had buyer's remorse after buying a new Cadillac. Her husband had only driven the plainest cars throughout their marriage. In a Grief Gathering, one participant gave her freedom with his words, "Lady, you need a good, dependable car. Sounds like you bought one, so enjoy it." Life does go on, so live it!

I can live my life now.

Make Some New Traditions.

We need traditions that help families deal with death, not just at the funeral but for months and even years after.

Mary Pipher, *Another Country*, p. 239

Tomorrow's tradition begins with today's innovation. In *Creating Meaningful Funeral Ceremonies* (p. 56), Alan Wolfelt suggested that "meaningful" traditions help grievers do several things:

* Acknowledge the reality of the death
* Move toward the pain of the loss
* Remember the person who dies
* Develop a new self-identity
* Search for meaning
* Receive ongoing support from others

Since hollow traditions complicate grief, sometimes grievers have to say "good-bye" to traditions that they shared with a loved one in order to accommodate new or altered traditions, which may or may not work.

For example, a deceased mother or father may have been the glue that held a tradition together. In my family, my father always dressed up as Santa Claus (although everyone knew it was Dad). He continued playing this role into his seventies. That first Christmas after he died, we passed the tradition on to a grandson, but eventually we abandoned it. It wasn't the same.

On the other hand, one family decided to create new birthday traditions as a way of taking birthdays more seriously. Before the presents were opened and the candles blown out, each person present voiced one thing appreciated about the celebrant. The new tradition facilitated a renewed commitment to "saying it now."

I can make some new traditions.

Make Special.

For many, traditional funeral rituals have lost much of their value and meaning. They are perceived as empty and lacking creativity. I myself have attended way too many of what I would term generic funerals –cookie cutter ceremonies that leave you feeling like you may as well have been at a stranger's funeral.

Alan Wolfelt, *Creating Meaningful Funeral Ceremonies*, p. 7

Making special is a fundamental human proclivity or need. We prepare special meals and wear special garb for important occasions. We find special ways of saying important things. Ritual and ceremony are occasions during which everyday life is shaped and embellished to become more than ordinary.

Ellen Dissanayke, *Homo Aethecticus*, p. 223

"When I die don't go to any trouble" or "When I die I don't want a big funeral" are common requests. For many, "trouble" or "big" translates into $$$$. Rarely do we say that about weddings, even though one out of two marriages fail. And then, funerals and memorial services are about as permanent a ceremony as you can have. Ellen Dissanayke insists, *"Without extravagant and extraordinary ways to mark the significant and serious events of our lives, we relinquish not our hypocrisy so much as our humanity"* (p. 139). We become a little less human when we settle for today's traditional ceremonies reduced to "let's-get-this-over-as-quickly-as-possible" and, in some cases, "just-get-them-in-the-ground" mentalities. Seriously, we are talking about laying to rest a human being not disposing of a corpse.

"Making special" is an invitation to "Come be with me in my loss." *"Funerals and rituals are social invitations,"* Wolfelt argues, *"which say, 'Come support me'"* (Lecture, 1999). The funeral, though, is just one step in a process of "making special" that may continue through the first holidays, through the first anniversary. By making special, you encourage others to make special: "Remember at Alan's funeral when they. . .?"

I can make special.

41

Make Your Own Funeral Wishes Known.

I have realized I will now be less afraid to die because you have done it first. Whatever is ahead will seem more hospitable to me because I will think of you as being there to welcome me in -- in one more act of hospitality of the sort you have offered me all your life..

Susan Ford Wiltshire, *Seasons of Grief and Grace*, p.145

When my wife died -- it was unexpected -- we had never talked about anything along those lines. I decided I would never put my kids through anything like that again. A week later I went to see the funeral director to make my arrangements, one of the best decisions I have ever made.

Fred, participant in a Grief Gathering

A funeral and a burial are two of the most significant financial expenditures most people will ever make -- and the most permanent ones. Yet, many adults never get around to planning for this inevitability. The Jewish proverb is right: *"We know we will die, but we keep hoping that we will be an exception to the rule."*

You have faced a death and perhaps have experienced the emotional and financial strain of an unexpected death. By making your funeral wishes known to family members, your attorney, and taking advantage of a pre-need plan, you eliminate a great source of potential stress for those you love.

However, planning does not have to be morbid or complicated. Simply state, "This is what I want, and this I leave to others to decide." Then, be sure people know your preferences and where relevant documents are located.

I can make my own funeral wishes known.

Meditate.

It's one of the great cliches in our society.
Don't just sit there—say something!
Sometimes the soul is benefited by just the reverse,
Don't just say something – sit there.

Harold Ivan Smith, *Holy Me*, p. 67

Meditation has long been widely used as prayer by grief-keepers. Meditation is a simple, inexpensive way to still our racing, troubled minds. There is nothing to buy, memorize, use, or wear. All a griever has to do is show up. Lorin Roche defines meditation as *"sitting here listening to myself breathe."* You probably already know how to meditate -- you just do not know that you do.

To begin, find a comfortable space or position and sit. Take some deep breaths. Slowly turn down the volume of the world around you. There are several ways to meditate. You may want to take a word like peace, mercy, or hope and softly repeat the word. Or you may want to softly repeat one of these "jump-starters:"

Thank you, God, for your faithfulness to me . . . in my grief.
As a griever, I need to pay attention to my grief.

What are the pay-offs for making time to meditate? Roche identifies several:

❖ Release and relief from the stress and tensions of active grief
❖ Sorting through thoughts from our daily lives
❖ Reviewing the emotions we have experienced during the day
❖ Brief moments of deep peace
❖ Moments to let go of old hurts

Do not make the mistake of attempting to control the process, to try to do it "right," or to police thoughts. Just show up!

I can make time to meditate.

Name the Name.

I hated that nobody mentioned her; it was as if she had never been. I know now that it was because our friends did not want to hurt us, but you don't think too clearly after a death. Georgie helped break the ice. At a football game George had taken him to, Georgie suddenly said he wished he were Robin. George told me all his friends stiffened with uncomfortable embarrassment. When he asked Georgie why he wished he were Robin, he said, 'I bet she can see the game better from up there than we can here.'

Barbara Bush, *Barbara Bush: A Memoir*, p. 46

'There is no one to call me Rosie anymore.' Her nickname was lost with the last of her friends. Her world had grown colder.

David Wolpe, *Making Loss Matter*, p. 5

I am always amazed by how quickly people begin "pronoun-ing" following a death. Even some grievers rely on "he" or "she" rather than the name. In fact, saying the name is taboo. "Whatever you do – do not say the name." Yet, many grievers report that listening to friends "almost" say the name hurts enormously. "I see them skid to a halt," one widower reports, "and sometimes even change the conversation or walk away." People need to understand that refusal "to name the name" compounds the grief of the one who has suffered the loss.

Remember this! A loved one is not "gone" until two things happen: first, you stop saying the name; secondly, you stop telling stories about the person.

Sometimes, the griever has to break the ice and say the name to help people understand that it is okay to say the name.

I can say my loved one's name.

Never Apologize for Crying.

I cry inside my head so no one can see.

Tommy, a child griever

Grievers in this culture are quickly trained to apologize immediately for tears. "I'm sorry," "Excuse me," or "Excuse my tears." One thing we try to do in Grief Gatherings is to empower tears: "No . . . do not apologize for being in grief."

Tears are normal. Tears are natural. Human beings are designed to cry. Therefore, why should a griever feel the need to apologize for something as natural as shedding tears? What a sad assessment for a funeral or memorial service: "No one shed a tear!"

Tears are the exclamation mark of grief!

I can cry without apologizing.

Notice Your Environment.

The day after Robin died, George and I went to Rye to play golf with Daddy, at his suggestion. As we drove out on the parkway, I was shocked that the leaves were at the peak of their fall beauty. I remember realizing that life went on, whether we were looking or not.

Barbara Bush, *Barbara Bush: A Memoir*, p. 45

If I'm confused, or upset, or angry, if I can go out and look at the stars, I'll almost always get back a sense of proportion. It's not that they make me feel insignificant; it's the very opposite; they make me feel that everything matters; be it ever so small, and that there's meaning to life even when it seems most meaningless.

Madeleine L. Engle, *Glimpses of Grace*, p. 160

Have you ever been "ambushed" by a sunrise, sunset, or an unexpected snowfall? For some, having no one to call out to, "Come quickly and look at this. . ." is a potent reminder of their loss.

Liz Carpenter, a widow, described a timeout in her grief as she looked out the window and noticed a baby deer in her yard. Although she was on a long distance call, she announced, "*I'll call you back, I've got to take this in.*" She explains, "*And I sat there for five full minutes gazing at the wonder of it all, reflecting that I had just learned how to move from loneliness to solitude. There is a vast difference*" (Elizabeth Harper Neeld, *Seven Choices*, p. 124).

There do come unsolicited moments when nature offers us exquisite slices of beauty which can be of great personal benefit: a breeze, a sunrise, a cloud, or a perfect sunflower that begs us to stop and pay attention and focus on grief. Healing can be enhanced by a glimpse at the wonders of our environment.

I can notice my environment.

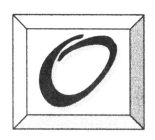 *Observe Memorial Day.*

*We call this day Memorial Day, a time to remember those
who've passed on. We'll remember, we tell ourselves, as we
mow our yards, catch a ball game, hit the stores. We'll
remember, we say, as we light the grill, pack the picnic basket,
and have fun with the kids. We don't remember--not the way our
parents and their parents did. The old ones, they still call it
Decoration Day. Decoration Day was about remembering,
remembrance reinforced by doing, remembering by decorating
graves.*

Mike Hendricks, "Remember the Point of the Holiday," p. B-1

Once upon a time, Memorial Day was a day to honor the dead. Now,
Memorial Day is, for many, merely the first day of summer. With the
decision by Congress to make Memorial Day a long weekend and the
mood to "get over grief," the observance has been altered.

Honor the day as a way to remember your loved one. The entire day
does not have to be spent in a cemetery, but the day is a great
opportunity to visit the grave or graves. For one reason, many people
will be in the cemetery, so you will not feel as alone.

Even if you cannot visit the grave, you can carve out a moment to
remember and to offer gratitude for the life of the deceased. From her
experience of grief, Melissa Gabbert says, *"Seize every opportunity to
honor the spirit of your loved one"* ("Holidays Without Mom," p. F3).

Amy Dickinson offers sage advice when you cannot visit the cemetery:
*"Teach your kids that Memorial Day isn't just about Kool-Aid and
wiffle balls. Before you stoke up the grill this year, raise a glass to the
people who came before you, those who fought for your country or
tended the home fires, and help your family celebrate the past."*
("Family Legends," p. 103)

I can observe Memorial Day.

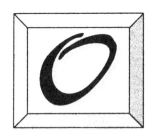

Overlook the Easy Answers.

The people who have helped me are not those who have answered my confessions with advice, exhortation or doctrine, but rather those who have listened to me in silence, and then told me of their own personal life, their own difficulties and experience. It is this give and take that makes the dialogue.

Paul Tournier, *The Meaning of Persons*, p. 191

I lost my mother in 1999. That is the way I am supposed to report it. *Lost?* Actually, my mother died. One way we try to "de-power" loss is by resorting to easy answers and euphemisms.

❖ It's all for the best.

❖ You never got to know her.

❖ She's in a better place

❖ It was a blessing.

❖ Best not to think about it too much.

❖ He is out of his suffering.

I am certain you recall others. Think of one or two of the easy answers or questions that ricocheted through your soul the first, fifth, or twenty-fifth time. I have been amazed by what people ask, "How old was your mother?" When I answer "eighty-three" I commonly hear, "Oh then, she lived a good long life," which sounds to this son griever like a disenfranchisement of my grief. "You shouldn't grieve too much," I am subtly told. "After all, your mom was old and had Alzheimer's."

I want to create a bumper sticker to place on every car in a funeral home parking lot: *"Thou shall not offer easy answers!"* Unfortunately, the reality is that some people do not know what to say. But thinking they are supposed to say something, they are tempted to "dust off" an easy answer. Sadly, they are unaware how those words make the griever truly feel.

I can overlook the easy answers.

 *Pamper Yourself.*

Treat yourself to the most pampering experience you can seriously afford – a week at a health spa, a cruise, a manicure, a haircut, a triple scoop of double Dutch chocolate ice cream. One survivor treats herself to something special every day--nothing too fattening or expensive--a pack of her favorite sugarless gum, five minutes on the drive home from work to watch the sun set in the Pacific.

Eva Shaw, *What To Do When a Loved One Dies*, pp. 282-283

"Take care." Two of the wisest words in the English language are two of the most ignored words. Individuals who attend a visitation or memorial service may say to the chief mourner, "Now be sure and take care of yourself." However, few, if any, hold the griever to any sense of accountability: "Tell me how are you taking care of yourself?"

Many grief managers wear themselves out looking after the needs of other grievers, especially children. They just want to bulldoze their way through all the responsibilities, decisions, and forms by reminding themselves, "I've got to get this done. . . before I can take a breather." Ironically, grievers, who are so good at caring for others, have difficulty receiving care and pampering.

Besides, who will take care of you if you don't take care of yourself? Maybe no one. Yet as one fast food restaurant reminds, us, "You deserve a break today," which loosely translates, "You deserve to be pampered." Treat yourself to extra moments in bed or to a long soak. Pampering does a griever good. As I suggested in *A Decembered Grief*, "Never apologize for choosing what will nurture you" (p. 24).

I can allow myself to be pampered.

49

Pay Attention to the Distress Signals.

One benchmark of a completed grief pattern is when the person is able to think of the deceased without [debilitating] pain. There is always a sense of sadness when you think of someone you have loved and lost, but it is a different kind of sadness – it lacks the wrenching quality it previously had.

J. William Worden, *Grief Counseling and Grief Therapy*, p. 18

Cars come equipped with all sorts of built-in warning signals and lights. If only grievers were so well equipped. Some grievers find that they have so much to do--particularly those who are serving as executors of an estate--that they ignore signs of stress and strain. Sometimes, there are so many details to micro-manage that it is tempting to say, "Just another hour . . . ," and we ignore the body's protests. What will it take for grief to get your undivided attention?

The body has a hundred and one ways to signal us: cramps, headaches, pains, diarrhea, aches, irritability, sleeplessness, indigestion, etc.

My friend, Dr. Frank Freed, often uses a wonderful question in counseling: *"What are you pretending not to know about _____?"* It is tempting to think, "Ignore it and it will go away." But the reality is that it may become far more complicated. Pay attention to the distress signals identified by William Worden (*Grief Counseling and Grief Therapy*, p. 25).

❖ Hollowness in the stomach   ❖ Tightness in the chest

❖ Tightness in the throat   ❖ Oversensitivity to noise

❖ A sense of depersonalization   ❖ Breathlessness

❖ Weakness in the muscles   ❖ Lack of energy

❖ Dry mouth

So what are you pretending not to know about your grief?

I can pay attention to the distress signals.

Quit Urging Yourself To Get Over It.

You may have heard – indeed you may believe – that your grief journey's end will come when you resolve or recover from, your grief. But you may also be coming to understand one of the fundamental truths of grief: Your journey will never end. People do not 'get over' grief. My personal and professional experience tells me that a total return to 'normalcy' after the death of someone loved is not possible; we are forever changed by the experience of grief.

Alan D. Wolfelt, Lecture, Olathe, Kansas, 17 February, 1999

Often grievers take on the "get over it" advice of a "grief-lite" culture. Grievers parrot the advice of a culture that has one goal: getting over grief as quickly as possible. I have had numerous widows say, "They tell me I should be over it by now." Those three words – *"they tell me"* – are enormously destructive because whoever comprises the "they" may never have experienced significant loss, or they may have been in a relationship that was unhealthy. One father told me, "Things do not get better. They get different." Things shift ever so slightly. Mark Doty observes, *"Things have shifted, with the passage of a whole year; and though sorrow isn't lessened, I'm in a different relationship to it somehow" (Heaven's Coast,* p. 283).

A griever needs to ask: "Am I getting wise advice?" Is this advice coming from someone who has "walked the walk" in order to "talk the talk?"

Barbara Ascher wrote after her brother's death, *"I have been trying to make the best of grief and am just beginning to learn to allow it to make the best of me" (Landscape Without Gravity,* p. 98). I will only make the best of me if I quit urging myself, "Get over it!"

I can quit urging myself to get over it.

Recognize Anniversary Grief.

*One woman buys her deceased husband a cow every year
-- she makes a donation to the Heifer Project, his favorite
charity. You might do something similar, donating the
same amount of money you have spent on your loved
one's gift.*

James Miller, *How Will I Get Through the Holidays?* p. 39

Sometimes, grievers report, "I don't know why I am so down . . ."
Then, after a few moments, the griever acknowledges that the day is a
red-letter day such as a birthday, or a wedding anniversary, or the six-
month or six-year anniversary of the death. "To the day" or some
variation is a common expression. My grandfather died on Christmas
Eve and for the next three decades, on Christmas Eve, my mother
would say, "I guess you remember what happened "x" number of years
ago today . . ." That is one reason a certain month, day, and year
appear on a grave marker.

Certain dates matter to our souls. The question is, "What do we do
with the anniversaries: honor or ignore?" Unfortunately, our culture
insists that we "get over" or "move on" and offers little support to
acknowledge an anniversary. As a griever, I am learning to turn down
the volume of the culture and to listen to my own heart. I encourage
you to find a way to honor the special day: perhaps some time alone to
remember, to reflect, to voice gratitude, to light a candle; perhaps
allowing yourself to freely roam the landscape of your memories, to
look at photographs; perhaps to reach out to another who also
recognizes this as a special day.

I can recognize anniversary grief.

Recruit Your Support.

You want to know who helped me? That's easy. It wasn't the folks with the answers or the folks with the cliches or platitudes or the advice. No.! It was those wonderful people who listened all the way to the end of my sentences even when my sentences did not have periods. It was those precious people who let me sob and slobber and wail and moan and who simply sat with me staring into the bottom of empty coffee cups as if the answers I needed might be hiding there. It was those who listened and nodded, patted and hugged, and wept and waited with me for this active season called grief to end.

Harold Ivan Smith, *Grieving the Death of a Friend,* pp. 107-108

Support for the grieving was once automatic. Upon notification of the death, people swung into action offering support to the griever. Our culture has changed. Neighbors may well be strangers. Furthermore, because some friends have never had a first-hand experience with death, it will be extremely difficult for them to be supportive.

Even today, while there may be strong initial support from family, neighbors, the church, and the community, within weeks or months, at best, that fades, and grievers are on their own.

Therefore, just as participants in a fundraiser "walk or run" often recruit supporters, so must grievers. Look around to see who is available. Then recruit them to be on your support team. Ask! Remember, some support by listening and others by offering advice or contacts. Some support by simply "being there" for the griever. Some, though, will fail to come through which causes grievers to often report: "One thing about grief is that you quickly learn who your real friends are." Robert Benson describes the response after the death of a friend's child: *"As the news spread around town, people began to do the only thing they could: they began to pray. Many of them did so with their hands" (Living Prayer,* p. 135).

I can recruit support.

Reflect on the Loss.

I walked by the bungalow (his mother's cottage at Walker's Point, New Hampshire) a lot this long Thanksgiving weekend. I found myself choking up. Then I found myself smiling. The agents (Secret Service) probably said to each other, 'the old guy's finally lost it.' But I couldn't help but think of the happy things and the sad things, but always at the center was Mum, stable, loving, kind, generous, thinking of the other guy . . . What an example she set for us all.

George Bush, *All the Best,* p. 578

Suppose I was to say, "Do not think about a hot fudge sundae. Just do not think about it. Put it out of your mind." By suggesting that you **not** think about it, you are now thinking about it. Who spends the most time thinking about grief? The individual trying not to think about it.

"Best not to dwell on it." That advice-phrase is a common disenfranchising statement. And yet, some friends will still tell you not to think about your loved one's death. But one mother who lost a 19 year-old asked, "How can I **not** think about him?"

One healthy way of dealing with grief is to reflect on the loss: both the primary loss as well as the secondary losses. For example, John misses not only his wife but also his breakfast partner – the one who cooked his breakfast most mornings. How does he confront that reality? "I try to remember the good times – all the good times. If a memory pops in – I just entertain it, but I do not ask it to sit down."

President George Bush deliberately reflected on his mother's death rather than trying to keep it at bay. What memory have you been ignoring? Memories do come "a callin," as they say in the South, because reflection is part of the healing process.

I can reflect on my loss.

Remember.

I'm convinced the reason we are here is to remember, if we understand memory to be that uniquely human ability to create from the past a sense of meaning in the present and a trembling sense of possibility for the future.

Student to Elizabeth Harper Neeld after the death of Neeld's husband, *Seven Choices*, p. 226

When I've lost people, I've found consolation in connecting their memory to things I regularly experience.

Mary Pipher, *Another Country*, p. 218

In a culture obsessed with forgetting, it takes a courageous act on the part of a griever to remember and to remember "aloud." To remember means to "re-member" or to reassemble our thoughts. *"Through active remembering, we restore coherence to the tangled, mangled narrative of our lives,"* concludes Robert Neimeyer.

Alan Wolfelt concurs. *"Remembering the person I have loved does allow me to slowly heal. Healing does not mean I forget. Actually, it means I will remember"* (Lecture, 17 February, 1999, Olathe, Kansas).

What exactly shall I remember?

- ❖ *The good and the bad?*
- ❖ *The bad and the good?*
- ❖ *The bad and the not-so-good?*

Always remember the "and" that links good and bad: the ordinary and the mundane, the "nothing much" seasons of our lives.

Remember all that made the loved one the loved one.

I can remember.

Ritualize.

We need more markers, rituals, and rites of passage for the old and the dying.

Mary Pipher, *Another Country*, p. 239

When words are inadequate, have a ritual. When in doubt, have a ritual. One way we acknowledge our grief is by reenacting or creating a ritual. One such ritual is the funeral, which, in some form or fashion, has existed for thousands of years because mankind felt the need to mark a death with some degree of ceremony. Funeral services provide for additional needs as well.

❖ They help survivors acknowledge the reality of loss.
❖ They offer ways to express our good-byes.
❖ They provide ways to offer support to the grievers.
❖ They give an opportunity to be with others who, too, have lost.
❖ They provide venues for promising future support and aid.

These days, grievers have an enormous range of options for traditional services as well as alternative rituals, or a unique blending of both. For some, the desired ritual is for someone "to say a few words." Others want the majesty of an elaborate religious service or, what one friend calls, "the bells and smells." Many desire something more in keeping with the life of the deceased. Whatever the format, a ritual is a timeout from the ordinary to offer recognition that something extraordinary has occurred.

Finally, remember that we do not get all our ritual needs met in one stop or one ceremony. There is a need to re-ritualize down the road. That can be as simple as lighting a candle on a birthday or taking flowers to the cemetery on the anniversary of the death.

I can ritualize my loved one.

Say It Now.

*The cab dropped us at Grand Central Terminal, and at the foot
of the grand staircase, we paused to hug and kiss good-bye.
My fear of flying prompted me to say, 'Fly safe,' and he
responded, 'I always do.' He turned to walk up the stairs and I
to enter the subway. But something compelled me to stop and
look back. A brief thought passed through my mind: 'What if
this is the last time I ever see him?' Little did I know this
premonition would come true . . . he was to be a passenger on
Swissair Flight III. Eleven and a half hours after we said
good-bye, his plane crashed into the waters off Peggy's Cove
near Nova Scotia.*

Lanita Hausman, writing about her husband's death in,
"Air Crash Investigation." p. B6

We keep assuming that tomorrow is something more than a wish. We walk around as if we have some piece of paper that guarantees us a tomorrow.

However, our days are made up of slices called "nows" which come in different sizes and shapes. Sometimes, a golden "now" presents itself and demands an act of courage on our part. This now is the moment to speak our truth, to get something off our chests. It is in tender *nows*, though, that we are given our best opportunities to end a feud, settle a fuss, correct a wrong, reclaim a friendship, or kiss away a tear. These *now* moments are wonderful times to say, "I am sorry . . . I was wrong . . . will you forgive me?"

So, say it! Even if it is a word at a time strung like beads on a necklace, say it. Even if you have to stop and resummon the courage, say it! Saying it now is the best alternative to regrets and "if only's" that complicate our grief. If my experience with grief – and with grievers – has taught me anything, it is the wisdom of this maxim: "Say it now!" The English proverb puts it accurately: *"Never put off 'til tomorrow what you can do today."*

I can say it now.

Sign Up for a Support Group.

Why would you want to hear other people's stories?
So I can have permission to tell my own.

Susan Ford Wiltshire, *Seasons of Grief and Grace*, p. 4

One of the safe places permission to grieve is granted is in aftercare programs. Often, funeral homes, hospitals, churches, and hospice grief counselors offer programs designed to help the newly bereaved "make sense" of their losses and their responses. These programs rarely provide answers, but they provide opportunities to ask questions and to interact with others that are also on the grief journey. They are wonderful places to discover you are not going crazy!

It takes a lot of courage, though, to attend one of the groups, for many grievers attempt to grieve Sinatra-style: "*I did it my way.*" But grief needs to be shared. Grievers need to hear "me, too" from other grievers. Thus, groups are often ideal environments in which to stumble toward resolution with the loss, as a result of sharing their experiences with others who offer support and encouragement.

When should you begin? Immediately or down the road? That is a decision you will need to make. Listen to your heart. Try more than one group because the makeup or style of a particular group may not meet your needs. However, do not base a decision upon attending one session. Go back.

I can sign up for a support group.

Symbolize Your Grief.

An idea, in the highest sense of that word,
cannot be conveyed but by a symbol.

Samuel Taylor Coleridge, quoted in Bartlett, p. 437

Symbols are a shorthand communication tool of the emotions; one symbol may be worth a thousand words. When in doubt, symbolize. Look at the power of the simple piece of folded red ribbon as a symbol for concern about AIDS or the pink ribbon for breast cancer. Consider the power of a folded American flag at a veteran's grave. Symbols are a way of communicating life has changed, sometimes radically and eternally, as is the case with death. Furthermore, the symbols people use tend to change through time.

Years ago, grievers were expected to wear black to the funeral. Widows once were expected to wear black for a full year. Now, with the growth in celebrations of the lives of the deceased, many avoid black or even dark colors and choose bright colors. Years ago, "mourning rings" were worn on the finger to symbolize the loss; black armbands were worn by gentlemen on their coat or shirt sleeves; wreaths were placed on the front doors of residences and businesses or offices.

Today, symbols have changed. People also do different things with jewelry. One widow took the diamonds in her wedding ring and had a jeweler remount them. Another had her wedding band redone as a cross and earrings, which she wore. She also had a pair of earrings made for each of her grown daughters.

The ways to symbolize are many and varied. Be creative and symbolize your loss. You may be amazed at how one simple symbolic act encourages healing.

I can find a way to symbolize my loss creatively.

Take Your Time.

Give yourself time. I have learned that grief is a journey.
Only you know what is right for you. Listen to your heart.

Melissa Gabbert, "Holidays Without Mom," p. F3

How impatient are we? Someone defined a millisecond as "the time from the light changing to green before the car behind you starts honking." We grieve in an impatient society. I often want to ask certain grievers, "What is the big hurry?"

"It's been five years," one widow informed the group. "Shouldn't I be over it by now?" Then she burst into tears. "It only gets worse," she said. I waited a moment and then asked, "How long were you married?" "Fifty-three years," she answered. "Fifty-three wonderful years." Amazingly, her children think that their mother should be over her grief for her husband as do many of her friends, some of whom have stopped calling, thinking that support is "enabling" her – as if grief were an addiction.

"Let's put it in a mathematical formula. If it took you fifty-three years to create this pool of memories, why would anyone think you could drain the pool in one-tenth of the time?" Many grievers assume someone has taken the relationship and set a timer on a giant clock. Eventually, the clock ticks "Ding" and your official time to grieve is over. What actually ends is the time family and friends willingly offer support. After considerable experience with grievers, I have come to understand that bereaved individuals will periodically have moments in which the grief returns like a cloud blocking the sun. Such experiences remind us that thorough grief takes time.

Impatience has hamstrung the grief of many persons. Take your time and do your grief thoroughly.

I can take my time.

Tell God What Is on Your Mind.

Sometimes when we're angry at God and galled at God's silence, the best we can manage to do is to confront God, confess our outrage, and risk speaking our minds . . . The journey from outrage at God to renewed affection toward God is long and bumpy. Praying honest prayers is the only example we have as our guide along the path.

Renita J. Weems, *Listening for God*, pp. 190-191

Many individuals have difficulty praying while in grief. Others have difficulty being honest in their prayers and conversations with God. How many conversations have you begun with, "So, what's on your mind?" Assume that God is asking you that very question. "God, if you are so powerful, why did my son/daughter/spouse die?" In my groups, I always ask, "Is anyone in this room angry at God?" Instantly, there is a cacophony of denials: "Oh no!" Then one timid voice says: "I am." Immediately, everyone spins to see who has spoken and to dodge the assumed incoming thunderbolt.

In reality, God already knows. My good friend, Dr. Reg Johnson, insists, *"God never chides his children for being children."* But why do we have to tell Him? Somehow, it helps us to put into words what is on our hearts and minds. Prayer is about honesty. Renita Weems reminds grievers, *"We do not have to be proud of our prayers or private conversations with God."*

I can tell God what is on my mind.

"Thumbs Up" Your Grief.

Whether it happens in one moment or over many years, losing faith deadens the spirit like a syringe filled with heroin or a line of coke. The most debilitating drug on this planet besides losing faith in God is when we stop believing in ourselves.

Melodie Lynn Beattie, *Stop Being Mean to Yourself*, p. 147

In real life, grief is a train that doesn't run on anyone else's schedule.

Ellen Goodman, "Mourning Gets the Bum's Rush," p. B7

Take a moment to look at your thumb. Look closely. All those lines and squiggles interact to make your thumbprint unique, a "one-of-a-kind-in-the-whole-universe." Not even an identical twin would have an identical thumbprint. If God went to that much trouble to make our thumbs unique, why would he want our grief to be "just like everyone else's." Maybe, just maybe, our griefprint should be equally unique.

One by-product of the "stages" of grief is that many people will think you should be doing grief in a particular manner or progression, particularly in making progress toward "getting over it." The reality is this: **You are the only one who can get your grief right**. You are the only one who can do your grief. So, in the absence of affirmation for your grief work, give yourself a thumbs up – in essence, saying, "Way to go."

I can give myself a thumbs up for doing my grief work.

Trust Your Loved One to God's Keeping.

For hope in eternal life is not some unverifiable curiosity tacked on as an appendage to faith but is faith in the living, creating God carried to its radical depth. It is faith in God that does not stop halfway but follows the road consistently to the end, trusting that the One who calls things from nothingness into being, can, and in fidelity does, call them also from death to new life.

Elizabeth A. Johnson, *Friends of God and Prophets,* p. 211

Some of the tenderest words of the funeral ritual are, unfortunately, said only once: at the committal. They need to be said again and again, especially in the midnight hours when our minds and hearts ache, when "What ifs" and "If onlys" make shambles of our clinging to peace.

Even though I have two doctorates in religion, there is much that I do not know and more that I do not understand about eternal life. As a griever, I have sat in puzzlement for hours, reexamining what I have believed and what I have been taught. On a cold Christmas Eve, I stood at a grave in Johnson County, Kansas, and read eloquent words that I believe to be true:

If the compassionate power of God could bring about the existence of the world in the beginning, and if the living God . . . is unshakably faithful, then that same compassionate power can be trusted not to let persons perish into oblivion but to engage in an act of new creation at the end. In this perspective, faith in the creating God gave rise to the conviction that the Creator Spirit keeps faith with the beloved creature even in death.

Elizabeth A. Johnson, *Friends of God and Prophets*, p. 210

I can trust my loved one to God's keeping.

Update Your Estate Plan.

I wonder about how many family fights happen because the dearly departed failed to execute a will and leave specific instructions about bequest? Please tell your readers never to trust someone else to carry out their wishes without specifying those wishes in black and white.

Letter to Ann Landers, "Leave Heirs a Legacy," p. F6

You do not know what kind of family you are in until you divide an estate. Money is not always the issue – a punch bowl will do nicely to launch a holy war. In a study of adults age fifty and over, the AARP reports that twenty percent thought an inheritance – or lack of one – caused hard feelings among members of the family. Why do tensions develop? Certain individuals think the division of property is unfair or favors one child; still other individuals suspect that the "will-maker" was influenced to tip the estate in someone's benefit; or children from a first marriage feel left / cut out.

Now that **you** have had this loss, you need to update your estate document to reflect the new realities and considerations. For many readers, I need to say, "You need to make an estate plan, now!" You may protest, "For what little I have?" The reality is that you may be worth more dead than alive, particularly if you die in an accident. Sadly, more than one out of two adults do not have any type of estate plan. The following items are only some of the reasons one definitely needs to have an up-to-date estate plan:

❖ If you envision a large estate (to minimize taxes)
❖ If you have children under age 18
❖ If this is a subsequent marriage for you and there are children or stepchildren from previous marriages
❖ If you suspect that one of your children (children-in-law) will want or expect more than their "fair" share

I can do myself, my children, my executor a favor and review and update my estate plan.

Visit the Cemetery or Scattering Area.

This cemetery is too small for his spirit, but we submit his body to the ground. The grave is narrow for his soul, but we commit his body to the ground. No coffin, no crypt, no stone can hold his greatness. But we submit his body to the ground.

Ralph David Abernathy, *And the Walls Came Tumbling Down*, p. 484

I have friends who call and say, "Just checking up on you." That is what a visit to the cemetery or scattering area is.

Do I go or not go? That question produces quite a lively discussion in Grief Gatherings. Many do go and then others have difficulty admitting that they go to the cemetery. However, once people know you go, they will want to know how often you go.

When do you go? Many people go on Memorial Day because they want their loved one's grave to be marked with fresh flowers to avoid a comment, "What would the neighbors think?" Some go to talk to the dead whenever they have had some good days – a habit of George Burns. There is little wonder that *Our Town* has been a perennial favorite of drama groups. I also know young males who have lost a pal, who go to the grave just to "hang out."

Furthermore, it is amazing what people take to the graves: pinwheels that spin in the wind, Teddy Bears, notes, cards, or flags. The incredible outpouring of "gifts" at the Vietnam Memorial in Washington, D.C., is giving people freedom to honor their dead in local cemeteries.

Finally, many find it equally important to visit the death site periodically. My advice is, do what you need to do. And if necessary, recruit a cemetery buddy to go with you.

I can visit the cemetery or scattering area.

Write It Down.

I made a list of things I have to remember and a list of things I want to forget, but I see they are the same list.

Linda Pastan, quoted in *Women's Words*, p. 236

I have found that one great friend for grievers is a stenographer's pad. In my own grief, I have experienced if it does not get written down, it gets overlooked or forgotten. If you were to read through my notes for a day, you might wonder, "Can't he remember anything?" Generally, I have had a good memory, but grief has a way of demanding more energy and more of my "storage." I find that I might remember when I get up, "Oh, I have a dentist's appointment today." But I also have discovered that I did not happen to remember it at two in the afternoon – at the time of the appointment – even though it was written on my calendar.

If nothing else, having a "to do today" list is a double reminder, especially if the deceased functioned as your back-up memory. Besides, it does help some days, just before bedtime, when I am tempted to ask, "Did I accomplish anything today?" Then, I can review my list and find something that I accomplished on what seemed like a wasted day.

If Santa Claus makes a list and checks it twice, maybe that would be a good example for grievers to follow.

I can enhance my memory by writing it down!

Write Thank-You Notes on Your Schedule.

Replying to and thanking people for their thoughtfulness when a loved one has died is more than good manners; it is a way to stay connected to family and friends.

Eva Shaw, *What To Do When a Loved One Dies*, p. 56

Society expects grievers to acknowledge the acts of hospitality that they have received.

Hopefully, someone has noted the flowers, the calls, the faxes, the e-mails, the casseroles, and the cakes. Where there has been a great outpouring, though, it is difficult for some to find the energy to respond. "Where do I begin?" Others see it as some "timed" requirement. "Got to get to those thank-you's . . ." Some find it a distraction from the loss, one of those "Keep Busy" directives.

The task can seem overwhelming if you have to tackle it alone. Therefore, you might do as some other people have done and enlist the help of children or even friends, particularly in the addressing of the cards or envelopes. If someone asks, "Is there anything I can do?" draft the individual as a personal secretary to assist you with the notes.

Give yourself time, even one note a day. If you are struggling with what to say, you can add these words as your expression of gratitude:

❖ *Thank you for thinking of me in this most difficult time.*
❖ *The kindness of friends like you has been a constant source of encouragement to me and to my family.*

I can write thank-you notes on my schedule.

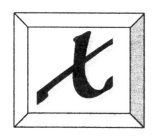

Xerox® Stuff.

It's here somewhere . . .
I just saw it the other day . . .
It has to be here somewhere . . .
Where did I put it?
It was just here!
Okay, who moved it?

Six good reasons to make photocopies of important documents

An executor's best friend is the photocopy machine. It is always wise to have extra copies on hand, starting with the obituary and service folders. Long after the number supplied by the newspaper or funeral home have run out, Xerox® copies are helpful.

As a griever, I have found that I need a "back-up" file. When I cannot put my hands on the original of some important document related to the death of my loved one, I have a Xerox® copy.

Additionally, in some cases, there have been notes I have received that I want to share with my sister who lives 500 miles away. I could read it to her on the phone, but somehow those words have a second life when she has a photocopy to read and to re-read.

Make a resolution to photocopy any important document including notes, cards, poems, etc., so that "Where did I put it?" and other such comments will not become regular components of your vocabulary.

I can Xerox®.

Yes! the Best.

At the time, we did the best we knew how . . .
At the time it seemed like the best, but now I'm not so sure . . .
It's all for the best.

Participants in Grief Gatherings

I constantly advise grievers, "Say 'Yes' to the best." In people's "hour" of grief, all kinds of less-than-the best and discount offers come along from individuals or companies who take advantage of their vulnerability. This is particularly true through phone sales. Interestingly, grievers have even found all sorts of things appearing on their doorsteps or in their mailboxes that they did not order. And then, grievers have found bills being sent for items not purchased or services not rendered. Grief is tough enough in and of itself without the added pressure of being subjected to the schemes of disreputable marketers of goods and services.

In grief, at times, it is sometimes difficult to know what the "best" thing to do is. It is easy to ask, "What should I do about?" or "What do you think I should do?" But free advice is not always wise advice. For example, some person to whom you ask one of those same questions mentioned previously might have also lost a mate, but she may have chosen a "lite grief," hence her responses are not based on the best experience. Others who offer advice have hidden agendas or ulterior motives. That is why it is best not to rush into doing anything, signing anything, or making any major purchases. The likelihood of a quick decision being best in the long run is doubtful.

And yet, still others will even challenge a griever's decision. Therefore, grievers occasionally find themselves defending their decision. Sometimes, it will be difficult to say "Yes" to the best. But it pays great dividends.

I can say "Yes" to the best.

"Zest Up" Your Life.

After I came home from the funeral, I walked through my house. Then I said to myself, There are going to be three rules around here from now on: Lots of light, lots of color, and lots of good smells. An hour later, I was at the paint store picking out the new color for my living room.

Ruth, a widow

Lively up your life.

Tee-shirt in Saint Thomas, Virgin Islands

Many grievers describe their loved ones as having had a "zest for life" or being "full of life." And that may have once characterized the griever as well, but they are left to wonder, "Will the sun ever shine as brightly?" Moreover, "comforters" are quick to suggest: "She would not want us carrying on like this . . or to be sad . . or etc." (Lots of etc.).

In time, though, you will again taste life. In a surprising moment, a bubble of joy will erupt in a long silenced corridor of the heart. Life is not over with this loved one's death, but it is different.

The tee-shirt implies that we do not leave it up to others to "lively up" or "zest up" our lives. So, what is something you can do to add some zest in your life? Think and do.

I can, in time, "zest up" my life.

Zoom In, Zoom Out.

Most mourners do not realize that they have a choice in how they heal from their grief. Grieving can continue as long as necessary, but, at the same time, the survivor can move into a healthy pattern of living.

Sandra Jacoby Klein, *Heavenly Hurts*, p. 119

These days even inexpensive cameras have a zoom feature that allows us to get close to or distance us from an animate or inanimate object. Some of the greatest pictures only happen with the aid of a zoom lens. My zoom lens, for example, offers me a chance to see some objects far more clearly than with my natural eye. Then, I can take a better picture. Grief also provides opportunities for us to use the "zoom" lens of our souls for clarity and definition. Sometimes, though, we get too close to the subject and need to "de-zoom." It is possible, in grief, to be "so close to the tree that your vision is blurred and you cannot see the forest."

For example, sometimes grievers need to take in the whole picture of the loved one's life. The way an individual's life ends, or circumstances in our lives at the time of death casts a shadow or cloud over other aspects of our loved one's life. Over time, we hopefully may come to see the loss with the proper perspective.

Additionally, comparing pictures we have taken with different lens settings might surprise us. We may not know of the impact a loved one had until we view the different pictures and hear the condolences and the stories that punctuate them.

Give yourself time and use different lens settings to provide yourself with a truer, clearer picture. Visions of varying degrees of closeness helps us see our grief in a different, healthier light.

I can take the high road by zooming in or zooming out of this experience.

Conclusion

You are a griever. Nothing will change the loss that has interrupted your life and made you a griever, so the question is not, "What will I do *about* my grief?" Grief is not a problem to be solved. It is an opportunity to be seized. Neither is grief a destination. Grief is a process. Therefore, the real question is "What will I do *with* my grief?"

When Jimmy Stewart's wife died, the great film actor "withdrew from the world." In his daughter's words, "*He didn't know what to do with himself,*" or with his grief. Four years later, in 1997, Stewart died. How much life he missed out on during those four years by isolating himself in his grief ("No Man Is Poor Who Has Friends," p. A-2).

On the other hand, the horrible death of Matthew Shepard put his family in front of the world media. They did not have the luxury of withdrawing from the world, as did Stewart. On the first anniversary of Matthew's death, his mother, Judy, had a chance to reflect on her experience. Her words may offer some hope to you:

The past year has been a learning experience for our entire family. One thing brought painfully to all our minds and hearts is that we take far too much for granted. We think that there will always be a tomorrow to talk, hug, discuss, settle questions, declare our love, share our ideas, and be at peace. We have found that this is not the case. We should never wait until later to share our feelings. Life is too short. At the same time, we realize the waste of energy in regrets. One can get lost in regret and forget about the wonderful, happy memories that are part of everyone's life. Grief is a very individual and personal experience. Everyone goes through loss in his or her own way.

Judy Shepard, quoted in *The Advocate*, p. 41

When you get ready

to leave those dark places behind

- - having well done your grief - -

leave behind

a candle and a match

for those who will next occupy

this sacred space

called grief.

Harold Ivan Smith

Sources

Abernathy, Ralph David. (1989). *And the Walls Came Tumbling Down.*
New York: Harper and Row.

Ascher, Barbara Lazear. (1992). *Landscape Without Gravity.* New York:
Delphium.

Albom, Mitch. (1997). *Tuesdays with Morrie.* New York: Doubleday.

Anderson, Margaret. (1996). In Mary Biggs (Ed.), *Women's Words:
The Columbia Book of Quotations by Women.* New York: Columbia
University Press, p. 218.

Bartlett, John. (1855/1980). *Familiar Quotations: A Collection of
Passages, Phrases and Proverbs Traced to Their Sources in Ancient and
Modern Literature.* Emily Morison Beck (Ed.). (15th Edition). Boston:
Little, Brown & Company.

Beattie, Melodie Lynn. (1997). *Stop Being Mean to Yourself: A Story
about Finding the True Meaning of Self-Love.* San Francisco: Harper.

Benson, Robert. (1998). *Living Prayer.* New York: Jeremy P. Tarcher/
Putnam.

Bernall, Misty. (1999). *She Said "Yes": The Unlikely Martyrdom of
Cassie Bernall.* Farmington, PA: Plough Publishing House.

Biggs, Mary. (Ed). (1996). *Women's Words: the Columbia Book of
Quotations by Women.* New York: Columbia University Press.

Boyd. Malcolm. (1998). *Go Gently into That Good Night.* Columbus, MS:
Genesis Press, Inc.

Bush, Barbara. (1994). *Barbara Bush: A Memoir*. New York: Charles Scribner's Sons.

Bush, George. (1999). *All the Best: My Life in Letters and Other Writings*. New York: Scribner.

Cook, Alicia Skinner, and Oltjenbruns, Kevin Ann. (1998). *Dying and Grieving: Life Span and Family Perspectives* (Second ed.). Fort Worth, TX: Harcourt Brace College Publishers.

Dickinson, Amy. (1999, 31 May). "Family Legends." *Time*, p.103.

Dissanayke, Ellen. (1995). *Homo Aethecticus*. Seattle, WA: University of Washington Press.

Doty, Mark. (1996). *Heaven's Coast: A Memoir*. New York: Harper Collins.

Edelman, Hope cited in Sorel, Nancy Caldwell. (1994, 15 May). "Grief Has No Beginning, Middle, or End." *The New York Times Book Magazine*, p. 723.

Finley, Mitch. (1996). *101 Ways to Nourish Your Soul*. New York: Crossroad.

Fitzgerald, Helen. (1994). *The Mourning Handbook*. New York: Simon and Schuster.

Gabbert, Melissa. (1999, 15 December). "Holidays Without Mom." *The Kansas City Star*, p. F3.

Goodman, Ellen. (1998, 6 January), "Mourning Gets the Bum's Rush." *The Kansas City Star*, p. B7.

Hausman, Lanita. (1999, 9 December). "Air Crash Investigation Is Too Important to Rush." *The Kansas City Star*, p. B6.

Hendricks, Mike. (1997, 26 May). "Remember the Point of the Holiday." *The Kansas City Star*, p. B1.

Johnson, Elizabeth A. (1999). *Friends of God and Prophets: A Feminist Theological Reading of the Communion of Saints*. New York: Continuum.

Jones, Wayne Lee. (1997). *Weave Garments of Brightness -- A Gathering of Prayers from Around the World*. NY: Berkeley.

Klein, Sandra Jacoby. (1998). *Heavenly Hurts: Surviving AIDS-related Deaths and Losses*. Amityville, NY: Baywood.

Lamott, Anne. (1999). *Traveling Mercies*. New York: Random House.

Landers, Ann. (1994, 6 July). "Leave Heirs a Legacy of a Good Will." *The Kansas City Star*, p. F-6.

L'Engle, Madeleine. (1998). *Two Part Invention: The Story of a Marriage*. New York: Farrar, Straus and Giroux.

L'Engle, Madeleine (with Chase, Carole F.). (1996). *Glimpses of Grace: Daily Thoughts and Meditations*. San Francisco: Harper.

Lightner, Candy. (1995). In Eva Shaw. (1994). *What to Do When a Loved One Dies*. Irvine, CA: Dickens Press.

Manning, Doug. (1979). *Don't Take My Grief Away*. San Francisco: Harper.

Miller, James. (1996). *How Will I Get Through the Holidays: 12 Ideas for Those Whose Loved One Has Died*. Fort Wayne, IN: Willowgreen Publishing.

Morris, Edmund. (1979). *The Rise of Theodore Roosevelt*. New York: Coward, McGann, and Geoghegan.

Murray, Carolyn Kresse. (1996, October). "Getting in Touch with Massage." *Nursing96*, pp. 32f, 32h.

Muto, Susan A. (1984). *Pathways of Spiritual Living*. Garden City, NJ: Doubleday.

Neeld, Elizabeth Harper. (1990) *Seven Choices: Taking the Steps to New Life After Losing Someone You Love.* New York: Delta-Dell.

Neimeyer, Robert A. (1998). *Lessons of Loss: A Guide to Coping.* New York: McGraw-Hill / Premis Custom Publishing.

"No Man Is Poor Who Has Friends." (1997, 8 July). *The Kansas City Star,* p. A-2.

Pastin, Linda. (1996). In Mary Biggs (Ed.) *Women's Words: The Columbia Book of Quotations by Women.* New York: Columbia University Press, p. 236.

Perret, Geoffrey. (1999). *Eisenhower.* New York: Random House.

Pipher, Mary. (1999). *Another Country: Navigating the Emotional Terrain of Our Elders.* New York: Riverhead Books.

Ponanski, Joe. (1999, 28 November). "Coping and Coaching." *The Kansas City Star,* pp. C1, C10.

Pooh's Little Instruction Book. (1995). Inspired by A. A. Milne. New York: Dutton.

Rivers, Joan. (1997). *Bouncing Back: I've Survived Everything . . . And I Mean Everything and You Can Too.* San Francisco: Harper.

Rivers, Joan. (1997, 15 May). Lecture. Fourth Annual National Conference on Loss and Transition, Springfield, Massachusetts.

Roche, Lorin. (1998). *Mediation Made Easy.* San Francisco: Harper.

Rosten, Leo. (Ed.) (1980). *Treasury of Jewish Quotations.* New York: Bantam.

Schlosser, Eric. (1997, September). "A Grief Like No Other." *The Atlantic Monthly,* pp 37+.

Shaw, Eva. (1994). *What to Do When A Loved One Dies.* Irvine, CA: Dickens Press.

Smith, Harold Ivan. (1995). *Death and Grief: Healing Through Group Support.* Minneapolis: Augsburg Fortress.

Smith, Harold Ivan. (1989). *The Gifts of Christmas.* Kansas City: Beacon Hill Press.

Smith, Harold Ivan. (1996). *Grieving the Death of a Friend.* Minneapolis: Augsburg.

Smith, Harold Ivan. (1997). *Holy! Me? The Single Adult's Guide to the Spiritual Journey.* Nashville: Abingdon.

Smith, Harold Ivan. (2000). *A Decembered Grief: Living With Loss When Others Are Celebrating.* Kansas City: Beacon Hill Press.

Tournier, Paul. (1975). *The Meaning of Persons.* New York: Harper and Row.

Veciana-Suarez, Ana. (1995, 19 March), "Grief Heals Slowly, But It Does Heal." *The Huntsville [Alabama] Times,* p. H5.

Weems, Renita J. (1999). *Listening for God: A Minister's Journey Through Silence and Doubt.* New York: Simon and Schuster.

Wieden, Judy. (1999, 12 October). "The Shepard Family Heals." *The Advocate,* p. 41.

Wiltshire, Susan Ford. (1994). *Seasons of Grief and Grace.* Nashville: Vanderbilt University Press.

Wiltshire, Susan Ford. (1999). *Athena's Disguises.* Louisville: Westminister.

Wolfelt, Alan D. (1999, 17 February). Lecture, Olathe Kansas.

Wolfelt, Alan D. (1997). *The Journey Through Grief*. Ft. Collins, CO: Compassion Books.

Wolfelt, Alan D. (1994). *Creating Meaningful Funeral Rituals: A Guide for Caregivers*. Fort Collins, CO: Companion Press.

Wolpe, David A. (1999). *Making Loss Matter: Creating Meaning in Difficult Times*. New York: Riverhead Books.

Worden, J. William. (1991). *Grief Counseling and Grief Therapy: A Handbook for the Mental Health Practitioner*. (2nd Ed.). New York: Springer Publishing.